Contents

Acknowledgements

Thank you to all the members of my Facebook Group, Traditional Wet Shaving, for all their support during the writing of this book.

Special thanks to Graeme Fraser for keeping me on track with his proof reading skills, help and advice. Graeme is an artisan who owns and runs ShedEleven Hand Carved Shaving Brushes. I have included an image of one of Graeme's beautiful brushes on the front cover and some more in the Artisan section of this book. Graeme, thank you, sir.

Last but most definitely not least, thank you to my wife, Theresa.

Cover photographs. Brush: Handmade by Graeme Fraser, owner of ShedEleven.
Razor: Hoffritz Cutlery New York, silver plated German Merkur 'slant', 2-piece.
Scuttle: 1950s James Kent Staffordshire Pottery 'Old Foley'.

Introduction to Wet Shaving

As with so many book introductions, you'll probably want to skip this and go immediately to the main pages. Please don't do so on this occasion. You've bought this book, so you must have an interest in, or questions about, traditional wet shaving. You're curious enough to want to read about wet shaving techniques and that's great, but you're going to have to learn to walk before you can run.

I'm the first person to admit that I'm not an expert, but I now know a lot more than when I started to shave with double edge (DE) razors 4 years ago. Indeed, in 4-years' time, I will know more about wet shaving than I do today. The old sayings, "you learn by your mistakes", and "you're never too old to learn", certainly ring true when it comes to mastering the art of traditional wet shaving.

There are no experts when it comes to shaving. Each and every one of us is an individual who has to find their own path to achieving the perfect shave, if there is such a thing. Wet shaving with a DE safety razor is a never ending journey of discovery. You will have good times, bad times, bloody times, sore times and times when you will wonder why you didn't stick with your boring old disposables and cheap cans of shaving foam.

Anyone who has never before shaved with a DE razor will have to adjust to a new way of shaving. It's no different from learning to ride a bicycle. You're going to have falls and scrapes but once mastered, you'll wonder what on earth all the fuss was about and why you didn't start shaving this way years before.

Instead of learning how to stay on the saddle of your bike, you're going to have to learn the very basics of wet shaving and what that entails. You'll master how to hold the razor, how much pressure you'll need to apply or not apply, the importance of the many directions your whiskers grow, your skin type and what creams or soaps you can use and which you cannot. You're even going to have to learn how to deal with the inevitable dreaded nick or cut and why an alum block and styptic pencil are just as important weapons in your arsenal as a razor blade and a shaving towel.

Patience is required with any new interest or hobby and shaving the traditional way is no exception. Wet shaving is, in fact, fast becoming a very popular hobby for men from all over the world. If you catch the shaving bug and fall down the Rabbit Hole, as we affectionately call it, there'll be no turning back for you.

Follow me and I will show you the way to the warren of wet shaving and, at the end of our journey, it will be up to you to decide if shaving the traditional way is something you'd like to continue practising for the rest of your natural shaving life.

Some examples of Rabbit Hole Symptoms. What can start as a new way of shaving can quickly turn into a very enjoyable but addictive hobby. This is just a small part of my collection of old and new shaving equipment, from brushes and razors, to blades and shaving history memorabilia.

What is Traditional Wet Shaving?

In simple terms, traditional wet shaving is about shaving with a non-cartridge or disposable razor. A non-cartridge razor can be a straight razor (cut throat), single edge (SE) or double edge (DE) razor. Shaving soap, cream or croap is used in the process and can be applied with or without a brush. Aftershaves, balms and colognes are optional.

I won't cover straight razor shaving in this book. If you've only ever shaved with a cartridge/disposable razor and take on a straight razor, you're very likely to cut yourself to such an extent that you will turn your back on wet shaving for good. Always become proficient with a DE razor first.

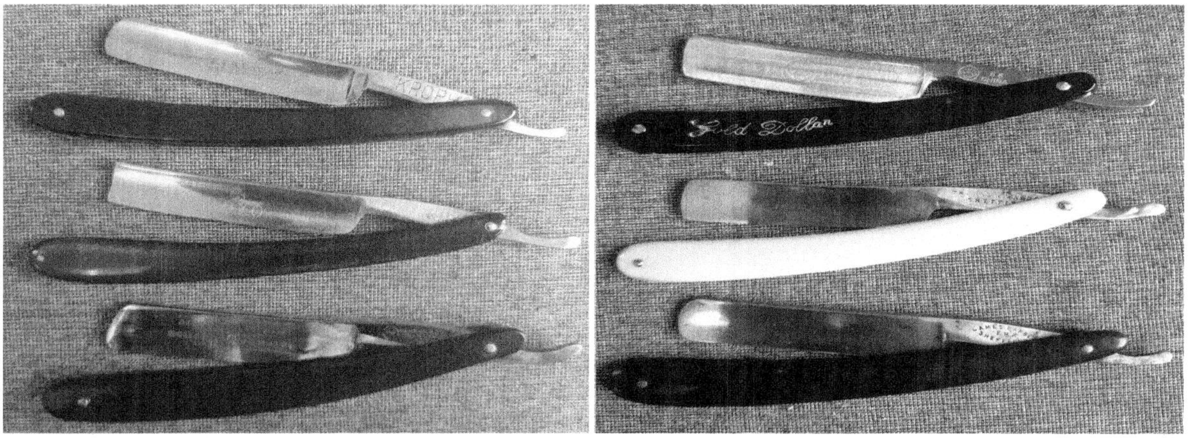

A selection of straight or cut throat razors. I do not advise beginners to even think about using one of these until they have used DE razors for a considerable amount of time and feel completely confident about doing so.

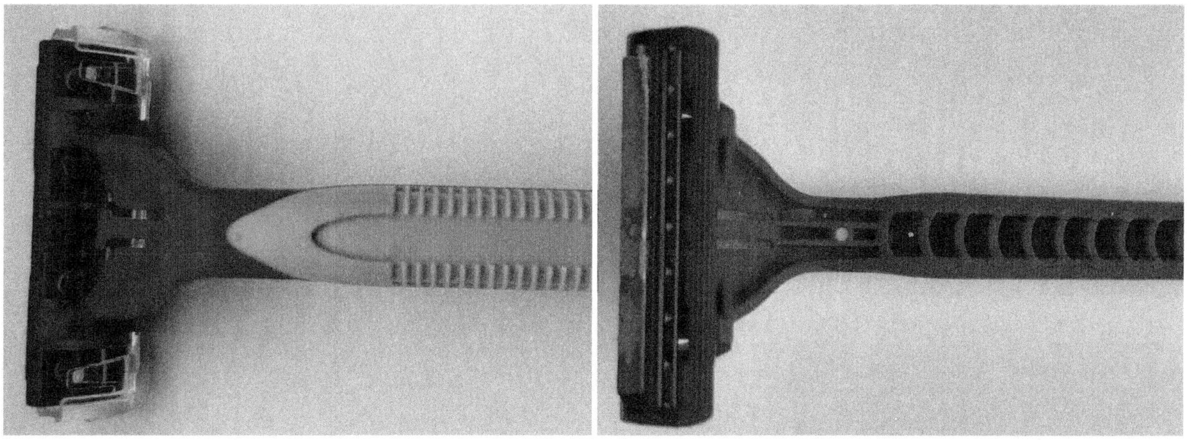

A swivel head disposable razor with two blades and a lubricating strip. Once the blades become dull, the whole thing is thrown in the bin and then resides in a landfill for the next thousand years or more.

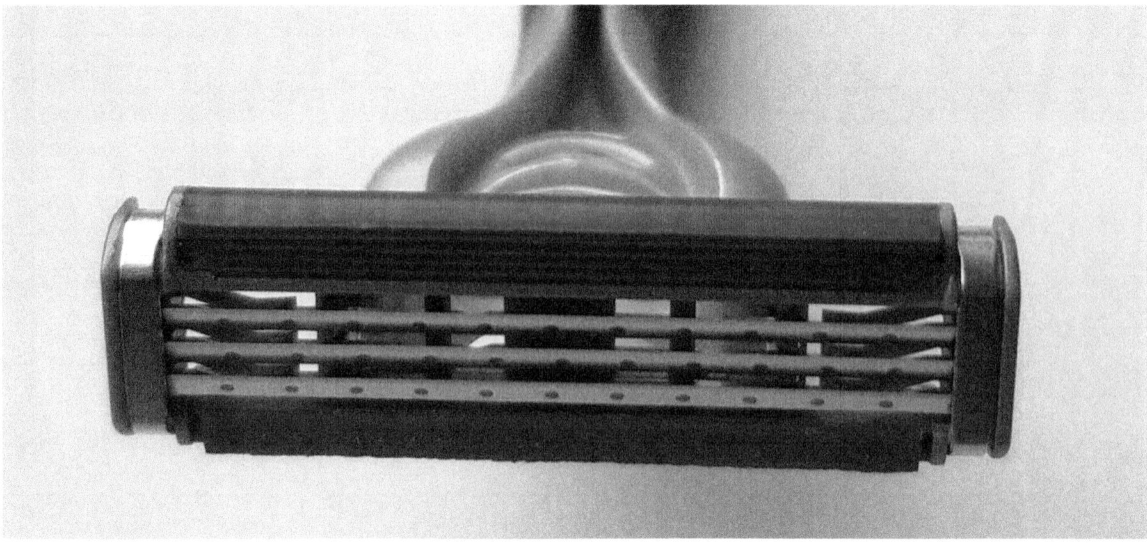

Above: A disposable razor with 3 blades. Multiple blades contribute to soreness and ingrown hairs due to the fact that so many blades pass over the skin in one swift motion. By the time the third blade arrives over the whiskers, it invariably cuts the hair underneath the skin; a perfect recipe for ingrown hair issues. When the blades become blunt, the whole thing is thrown away and more often than not ends up in a landfill site, where it will remain forever.

Below: A modern 2-piece Merkur 34C DE safety razor. The 34C is one of the best razors for beginners. It's reasonably priced, beautifully balanced and provides a mild but effective shave. When a DE blade becomes blunt, it can be recycled, so therefore it is extremely environmentally friendly. The 34C is the first DE razor I bought and it started me off on my journey down the Rabbit Hole.

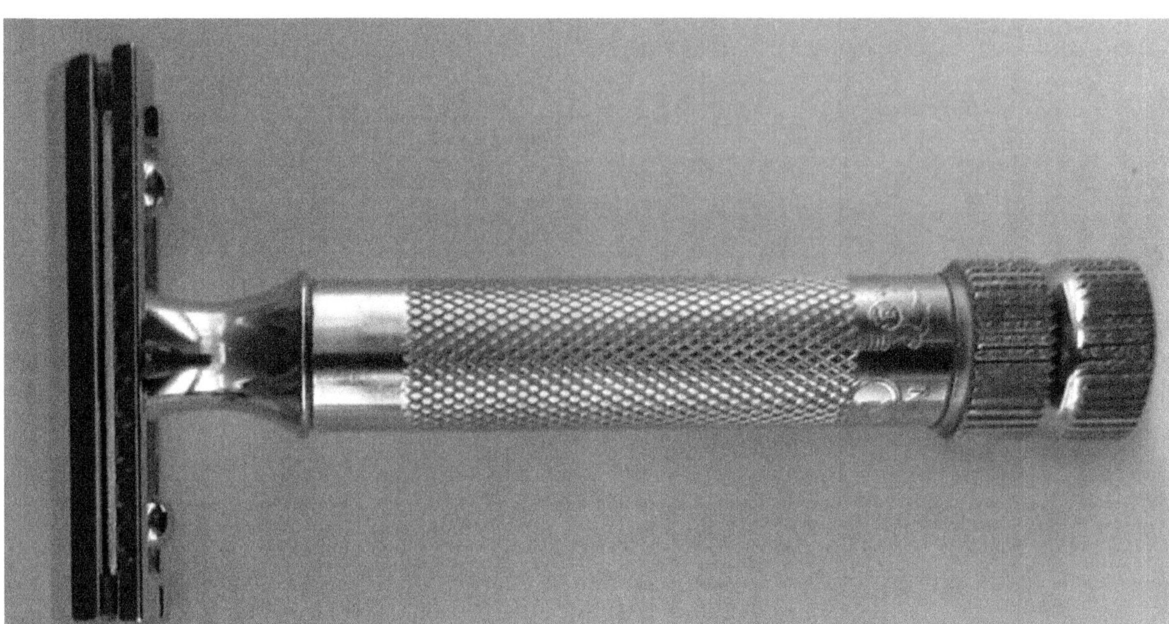

Above: The 34C disassembled into its 2 parts. The cap is on the left, the handle and baseplate on the right.

Below left: ASTRA blade packet and blade. The ASTRA is a great razor blade to start with and is available on the internet at very reasonable prices. It will provide at least 3 good shaves before it becomes dull and needs to be replaced.

Below right: The 34C is loaded with the ASTRA blade and ready to shave with. Notice the overhang of the razor blade (circled in red) which newbies and seasoned wet shavers alike should always be aware of. I'll explain more later.

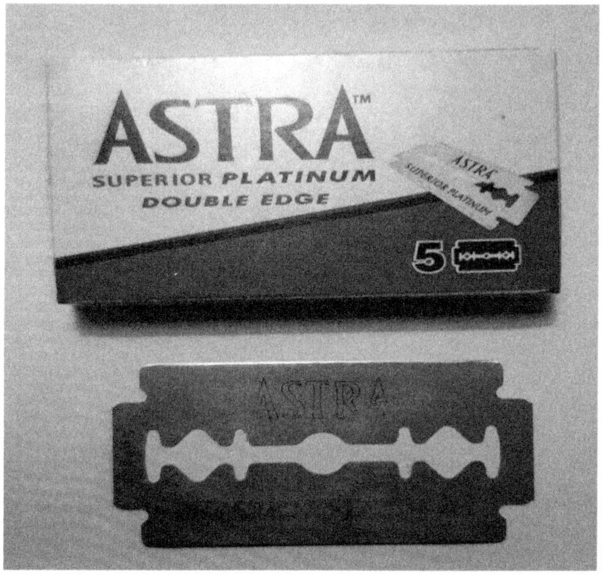

The Advantages of DE/SE Razors

There are many advantages to using a DE razor and just as many reasons why men and women all over the world are changing over from disposable and cartridge razors to join an ever growing band of people who have embraced traditional wet shaving as part of their everyday grooming rituals and routines.

I've listed below what I believe are some of the main reasons for using a DE/SE razor. Those I think deserve more explanation I have marked with an asterisk (*) and will be covered in a little more depth later in the book.

I haven't numbered the reasons or put them in any particular order because, as I stated in the introduction, we are all individuals and our opinions and experiences vary from person to person.

A Few Advantages of DE/SE Shaving

- **Environmentally friendly**
- **Kinder on the skin**
- **Cheaper***

I did say I'd list a 'few' of the main reasons. There are, of course, many more but, as we wet shavers like to say, "your mileage may vary", or YMMV for short. The fact is that you will have to decide for yourself what are or indeed what aren't the advantages of crossing over to DE shaving. You might give it your best shot and hate it. On the other hand, you may decide that it's the best thing you did since giving up smoking or taking up yoga classes.

Remember: YMMV

You have probably noticed that I have put a * next to 'Cheaper' and I daresay you're asking why I should do such a thing when I'm writing a book about traditional wet shaving. Please let me explain on the next page.

Will Shaving with a DE Save You Money?

There are two answers to this question: yes and no. Shaving with a DE razor and double edge razor blades can save you a fortune or cost you fortune. It all boils down to how far you fall down the already highlighted, infamous Rabbit Hole of wet shaving.

Before we get close to the Rabbit Hole, let's get down to basics and consider the aforementioned Merkur 34C 2-piece DE razor and ASTRA razor blades to compare the costs.

At the time of writing this book in December 2021, the Merkur 34C is available online for around £35. A pack of 100 ASTRA razor blades can be purchased, also online, for around £9-£10.

As I've already said, an ASTRA razor blade will give you at least 3 good shaves before it needs to be replaced. Again, YMMV.

Let's do some very simple arithmetic.

100 x 3 = 300. So that's 300 shaves for £9-£10.

Now let's compare that with the current price online for replacement cartridges of a very popular plastic razor that you can also buy online. I won't mention the make or model but you'll be able to work that out for yourself if you look at the picture on page 5 of this book.

Again, at the time of writing this book in December 2021, it will cost you around £8 for 4 cartridges.

For a fair comparison, let's say you get 3 shaves from your cartridge before the blades dull and clog, the lubricating strip dries up and you have no choice but to replace it with a fresh one.

4 x 3 = 12 shaves for £8.

Of course, you will have to purchase the razor in the first place. Once again, as I write, it will cost you online around £5.50 for the handle and they'll throw in one cartridge for 'free'. The manufacturer 'assures' us that each cartridge will give you 15 shaves. Hmm. Perhaps I was wrong, then.

Once again, YMMV.

I'm no mathematician or man of business but even I can work out that 300 or more shaves (YMMV) with a DE razor for an initial outlay of £35 for the razor and £9-£10 the blades ain't a bad deal.

Yes, you can and will save a lot of money if you buy a DE razor that will last you for the rest of your life. DE blades are cheap and will provide you with excellent shaves that are good for your skin as well as your wallet.

So why did I use the * in the table, I hear you ask?

Suffice to say at this moment in time that my explanation will take us ever closer to the mouth of the Rabbit Hole. In the meantime, please feast your eyes on some vintage DE and SE safety razors. All the razors are part of my ever-growing collection. Below are some vintage razors that I still shave with on a regular basis.

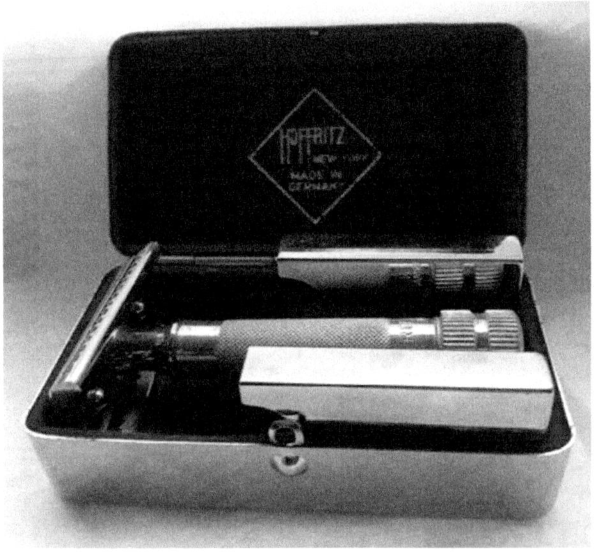

Do you like the razors on the previous page? Stylish, aren't they? If you like that sort of thing, of course. If you *do* like 'that sort of thing', I think you'll agree with me that they're very easy on the eye. For me though, the best thing about them is the fact that they're in perfect working order. I shave with each and every one of them whenever it pleases me to do so, which is quite often. They can all be loaded with brand new DE or SE blades that are are easily available to purchase online. I can honestly say that I've never bought a vintage razor that I can't use.

Below are examples of razors that were kindly given to me by family and friends over the years. They're pieces that I've never used to shave with. The blades they utilise can be purchased online from sites like Ebay and Etsy but would still need to be restored and/or honed by a professional before I'd put them anywhere near my skin. Instead, I proudly display them in my cabinet for all to see.

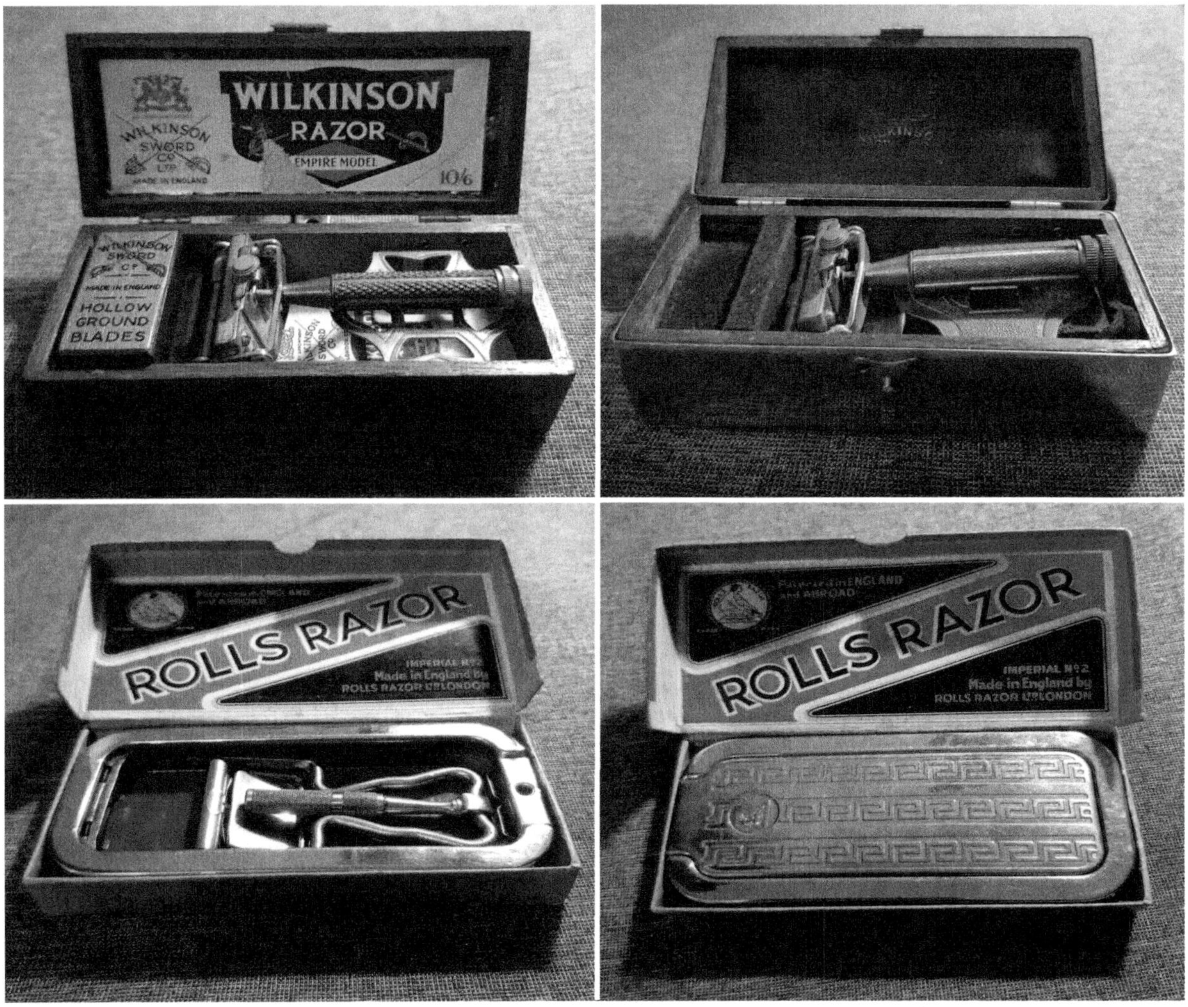

Starting Out

Basic Equipment

It's time to stop bunnying and cut to the chase. I've listed below the items you will need to set yourself up in traditional wet shaving. You only need to buy one DE razor and, if you look after it properly, you'll never have to buy another one for the rest of your life. Just imagine never having to buy a razor ever again. In fact, if looked after properly, a DE razor can be passed down through the generations and become a family heirloom. It won't necessarily gain in monetary value but it's sentimental value will prove to be priceless.

You will have to replace the consumables now and then, i.e. blades and shaving soap/cream, but they can be bought at very reasonable prices in supermarkets and online. Remember, a pack of 100 DE razor blades will give you 300 or more good shaves.

If you look after your shaving brush, your shaving brush will look after you. By simply rinsing and drying it properly after each use, it will serve you well for many years. In fact, a boar bristle will become more efficient over time and I'll explain how and why in later pages of this book.

8 Items of Basic Shaving Equipment

1. **New or vintage DE razor.**
2. **Shaving brush: boar bristle, horse hair, boar/horse mix or synthetic.**
3. **Shaving cream or shaving soap.**
4. **Pack of razor blades.**
5. **Shaving bowl.**
6. **Alum block.**
7. **Styptic pencil.**
8. **Aftershave balm - aftershave is optional.**

DE Razors and Blades

2-Piece and 3-Piece DE Razors

The descriptions of DE razors are pretty self-explanatory, and so therefore I won't insult your intelligence by going into too much detail. Suffice to say that 2-piece razors break down into 2 pieces and 3-piece razors into 3 pieces. A picture paints a thousand words, someone once said, so let's learn from the following photographs.

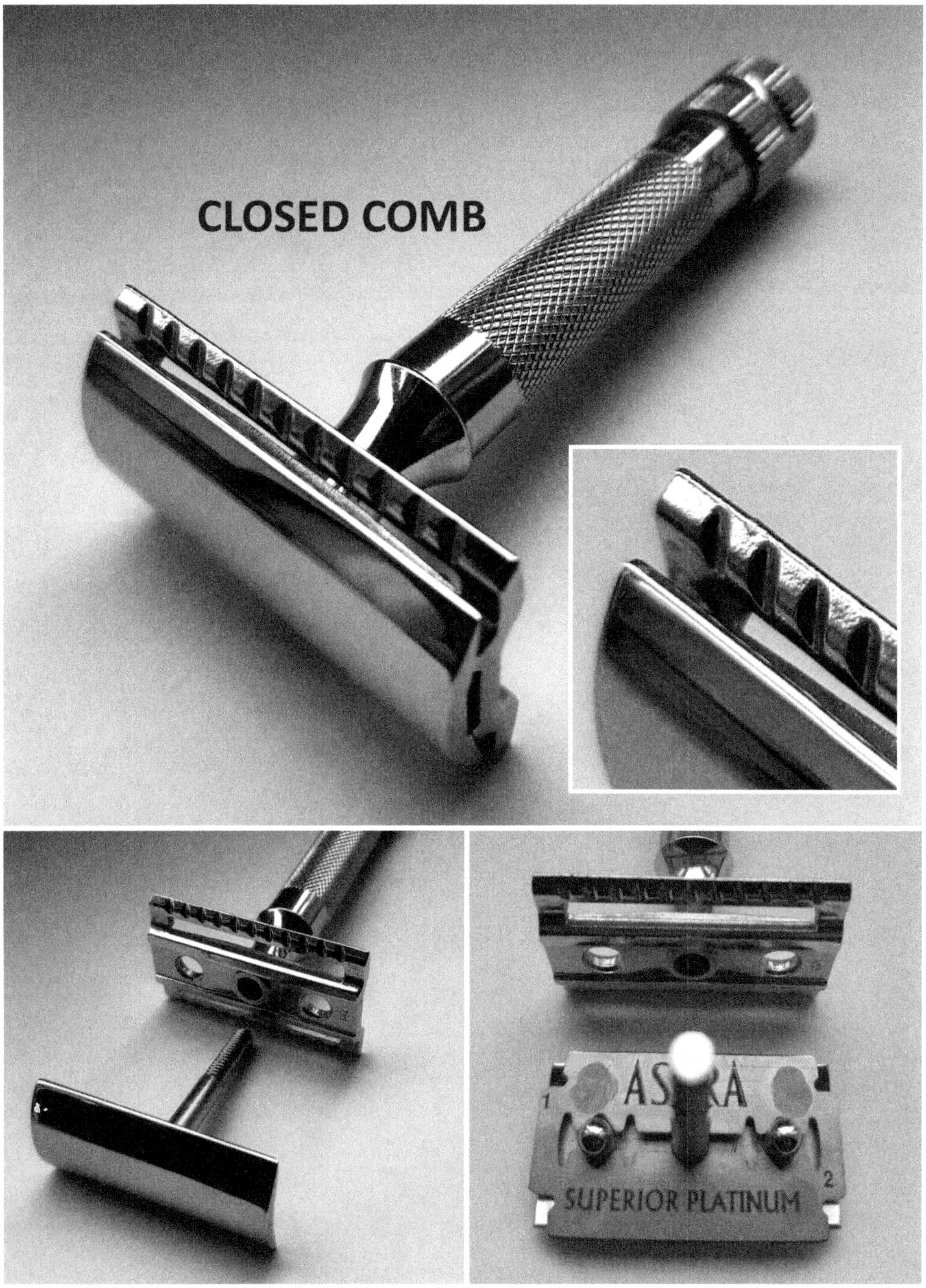

The Merkur 34C (pictured) is a closed comb, 2-piece, DE razor.

An example of a very collectable vintage ABC Pocket Edition Gillette open comb 3-piece. This razor is well over 100-years-old, takes a standard DE razor blade and shaves closely and smoothly but it's not one for newbies.

Open Comb vs Closed Comb

When you venture down the Rabbit Hole, you'll inevitably read and hear stories about how open comb razors are more aggressive than closed combs. From my own experience, I think that this is a load of old codswallop and should be taken with a very large pinch of YMMV.

Combs, whether they be open or closed, don't cut whiskers or skin. Razor blades do the cutting and slicing. If it were all down to combs doing the cutting, we'd have no need for razor blades, would we?

Open combs look more aggressive than closed combs, probably because their teeth appear menacing, but this actually isn't the case in real life.

In fact, I'm going to put my reputation on the line and say that I believe open combs are safer than closed combs, especially for men with thick, coarse and unruly (curly) whiskers.

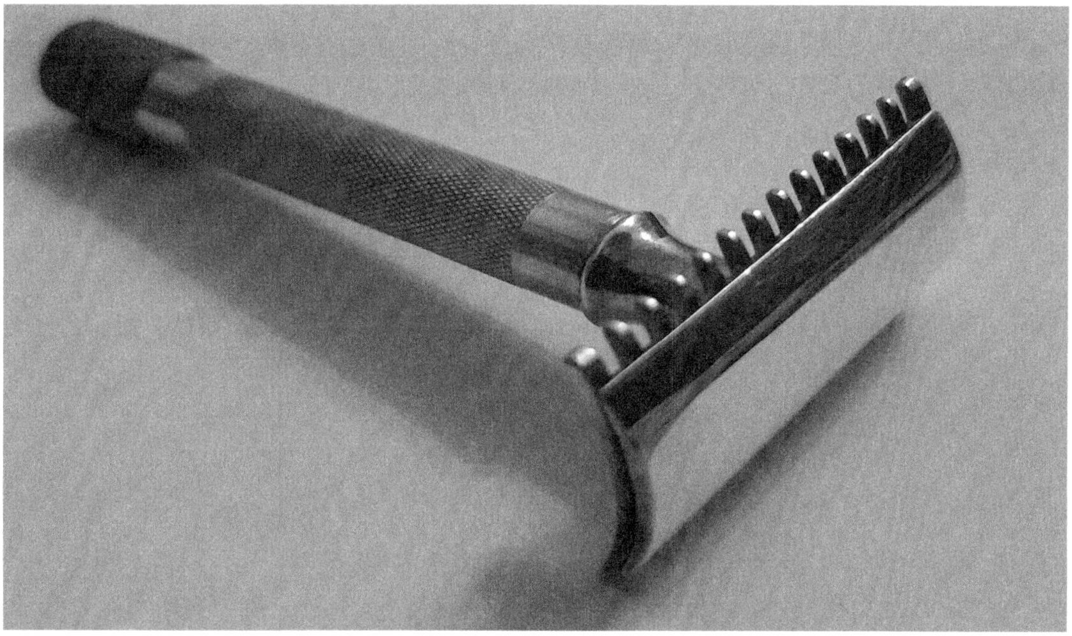

A vintage, silver plated, open comb Gillette single ring 'old type'.

Open combs do exactly what their name tells you. They comb through your whiskers and lather to open up a clear path for the razor blade to pass through. They don't clear away all of the lather, only that which is surplus to requirements. If your lather is good, sufficient residue will remain.

DE Razor Blades

Double edge (DE) razor blades are those with two sharp cutting edges. Both edges of the blade are used in a wet shave. When one side of the razor becomes covered in lather and whiskers, it's turned in the hand so that the clean edge of the blade can then be utilised. This means that you don't have to keep rinsing the razor every time one side becomes clogged, which saves time and provides as much use of the blade as possible.

Razor Blade Aggression, Mix & Match

There are literally hundreds of different brands of razor blades that can be bought online. When you are starting out, the best thing to do is purchase a pack of assorted blades and see how you get on with each one. Be sure to try them all in the same razor to give yourself an idea of the differences. Remember, YMMV.

The general rule of thumb is that aggressive razors give more comfortable shaves when they are loaded with mild blades and mild to medium razors do the same with sharper blades. Of course, when you get deeper into the Rabbit Hole and gain more confidence, you'll start trying sharp blades with aggressive razors and so forth. Pictured below is the famous Japanese Feather blade, considered by many wet shavers to be the sharpest razor blade in the world.

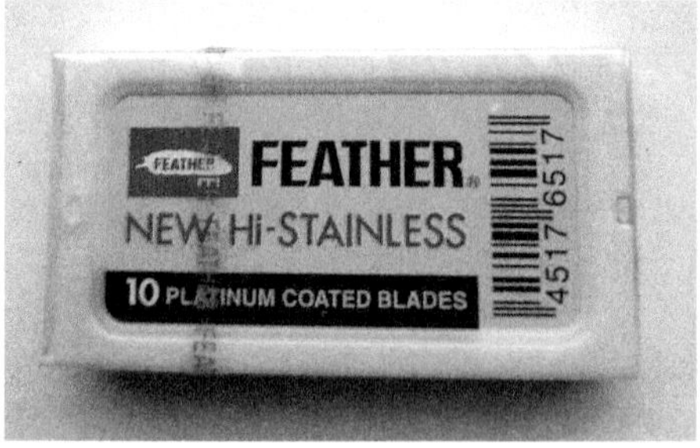

I would not recommend newbies to start off with a Feather razor blade. It is very sharp and unforgiving, especially when loaded into an aggressive razor like the Mühle R41. Very sharp blades such as these should be coupled with mild to medium razors like our old friend, the Merkur 34C.

Blade Exposure, Angle and Blade Gap

So what makes a razor mild, medium or aggressive? I hear you ask. Held in inexperienced or slippery hands, *all* razors are aggressive, even razors that are considered to be mild by shaving enthusiasts. Shaving technique has a lot to do with how you deal with aggression but there are 3 very important factors which must be taken into account.

Blade Exposure and Overhang

Blade exposure is how much of the razor blade you can see sticking out from underneath the razor cap. This has little to do with aggression, in my opinion, but many enthusiasts will and *do* disagree with me. YMMV. Overhang consists of the two exposed, short edges of the razor blade and, even though it is not sharpened like the cutting edges, will give you a nasty scratch if you catch it on your finger or face.

Blade Gap

Blade gap is at the sharp end of the business and determines how aggressive a razor really is. It's determined by the size of the gap between the cutting edge of the razor blade and the guard. The deeper the gap, the less protection your skin will have.

Blade Angle

Blade angle is determined by how much the blade is bent by the razor cap. The steeper the angle, the more aggressive the razor will be.

Both ends of the spectrum, side by side. Left Merkur 34C. Right: Mühle R41. The 34C is a mild to medium aggression razor. The R41 is an aggressive razor. Notice that the 34C has more blade exposure and overhang than the R41 which proves that blade exposure has very little to do with aggression.

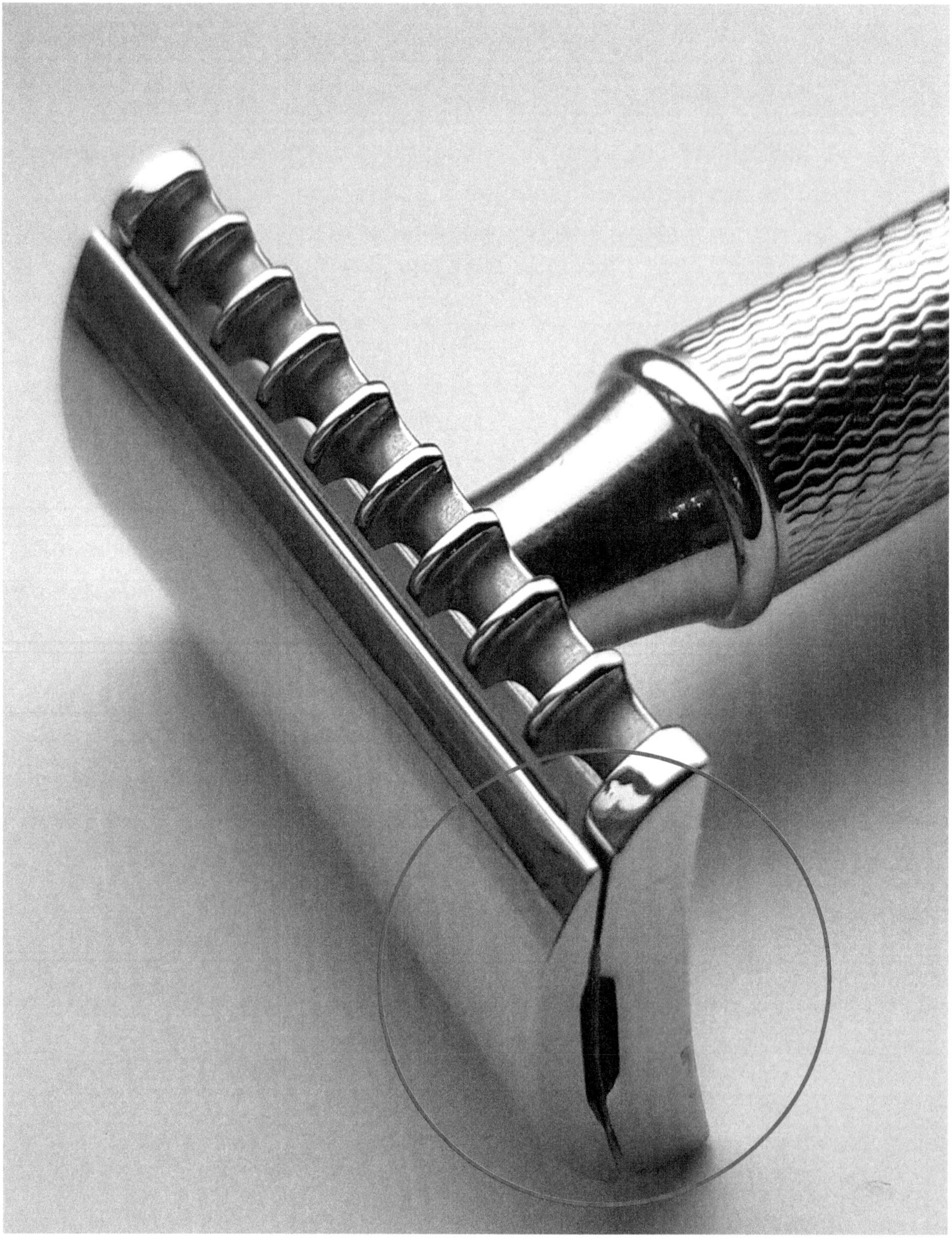

Above: A very aggressive combination. The Merkur R41 loaded with a Japanese manufactured Feather razor blade. The razor cap has bent the blade into a steep angle. The gap between the blade and the guard is also quite considerable.

This combination of razor and blade is not one that I would recommend that newbies attempt. Even experienced wet shavers would think very carefully before attempting to shave this way.

Used Razor Blades' Safe Storage and Recycling

Used Razor Blade Storage/Recycling

One of the best advantages of wet shaving with DE and SE razor blades is the fact that used blades can be stored away safely and recycled when the appropriate time comes, i.e. when your used blade bank is full to bursting. Instead of ending up rusting in a landfill site for the rest of time that is the unfortunate fate of cartridge and disposable plastic razors, DE and SE blades can be melted down and made into something useful.

I know of one particular enthusiast who is saving up his razor blades in order to one day melt them down and forge the steel into his very own straight razor blade. Of course, it will take many years before he is able to do so, but what a fantastic achievement it will be one day.

Storing Used Razor Blades

The best way to store used razor blades is to convert an empty food tin into a blade bank. This is very easy to do by attaching a circular piece of cardboard over the mouth of the can and creating a slit through which you can insert the blades. I made my own in a matter of minutes and it still isn't full after 4-years of wet shaving. Perhaps one day, I too will own my very own straight razor with a blade forged from my used DE blades.

If you have no inclination to forge your own straight razor blade, you can always recycle them. Ask your local authority for information on how this can be achieved and do your bit to help the environment.

Landfill. The final resting place for disposable razors. Photo courtesy of Tom Fisk.

NEVER DEPOSIT USED BARE RAZOR BLADES INTO YOUR RUBBISH BIN

Not only will the blade end up in landfill, it will also pose a serious health risk to not only you and your family, but to refuse collectors, refuse sorters and wildlife.

If you really can't find a few minutes in your busy day to make a simple blade bank, make sure you wrap the blade several times in sticky tape before depositing it in your internal and/or external bin.

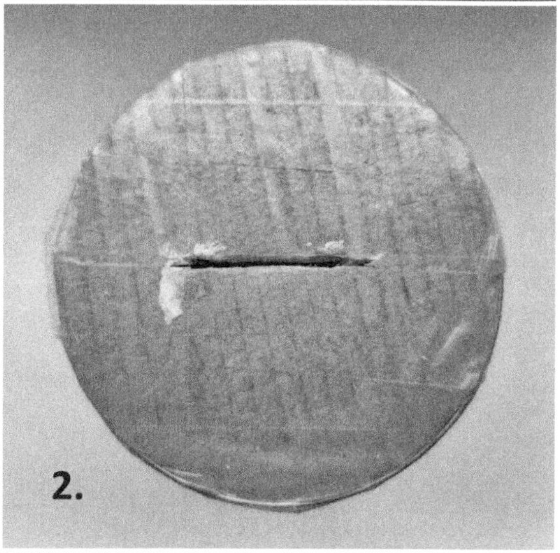

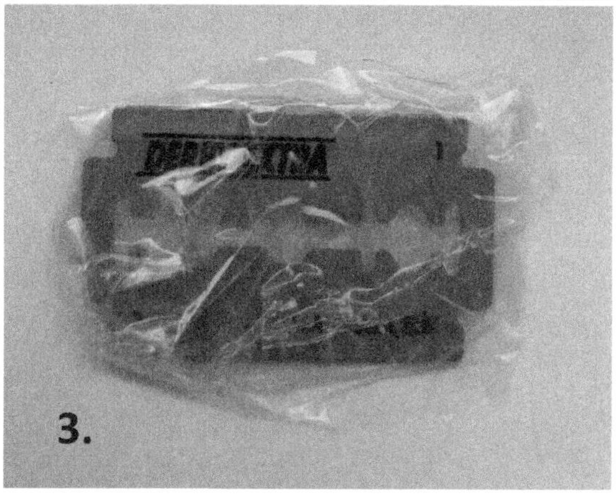

1. Blade bank made from an old food tin. 2. Top view showing cardboard and slit.
3. A used blade wrapped in sticky tape ready to be put in the bin for landfill.

SE Razors and Blades

SE Razors and Blades

Single edge (SE) razor blades are, I expect you've already worked out for yourself, razor blades with a single cutting edge. I'm going to concentrate on GEM blades because they are sold on the internet and are by far the best SE blades on the market. I own quite a few vintage SE razors and only ever load them with GEMs.

WARNING: DO NOT EVER use single edge razor blades that are not specifically manufactured for use in SE razors. Don't feel tempted to buy inferior blades that are designed for scraping off paint from windows. If you do, you'll cut and scrape your face to pieces in no time. They might look the same but they most definitely are NOT!

If you're intent on venturing down the Rabbit Hole, there'll probably come a time when you'll want to experiment with vintage SE razors.

Vintage SE razors take quite a lot of practice to get used to, so I don't advise newbies to try until they have become proficient with aggressive DE razors. If you do, you probably won't enjoy the experience and be glad you bought that alum block and styptic pencil. At worst, you'll be even more grateful that you live close to an accident & emergency department.

Okay, perhaps I'm exaggerating about the A&E department but it's better to err on the side of caution than to end up with a cut that won't stop bleeding and/or a scar that will last a lifetime and earn you the nickname 'Scarface' or 'Al Capone'.

Shaving with a vintage SE razor is about as close as you're going to get to shaving with a straight razor. One pass is usually enough to leave you with a very smooth face indeed. These razors were designed to do a good job in one pass, before the term BBS (baby bum smooth) had even been thought of by somebody, somewhere.

Keep the razor as flat as possible to your face when you first start out and adjust the angle accordingly. I cannot stress enough that these razors will give you a very nasty cut if you go in at too steep an angle.

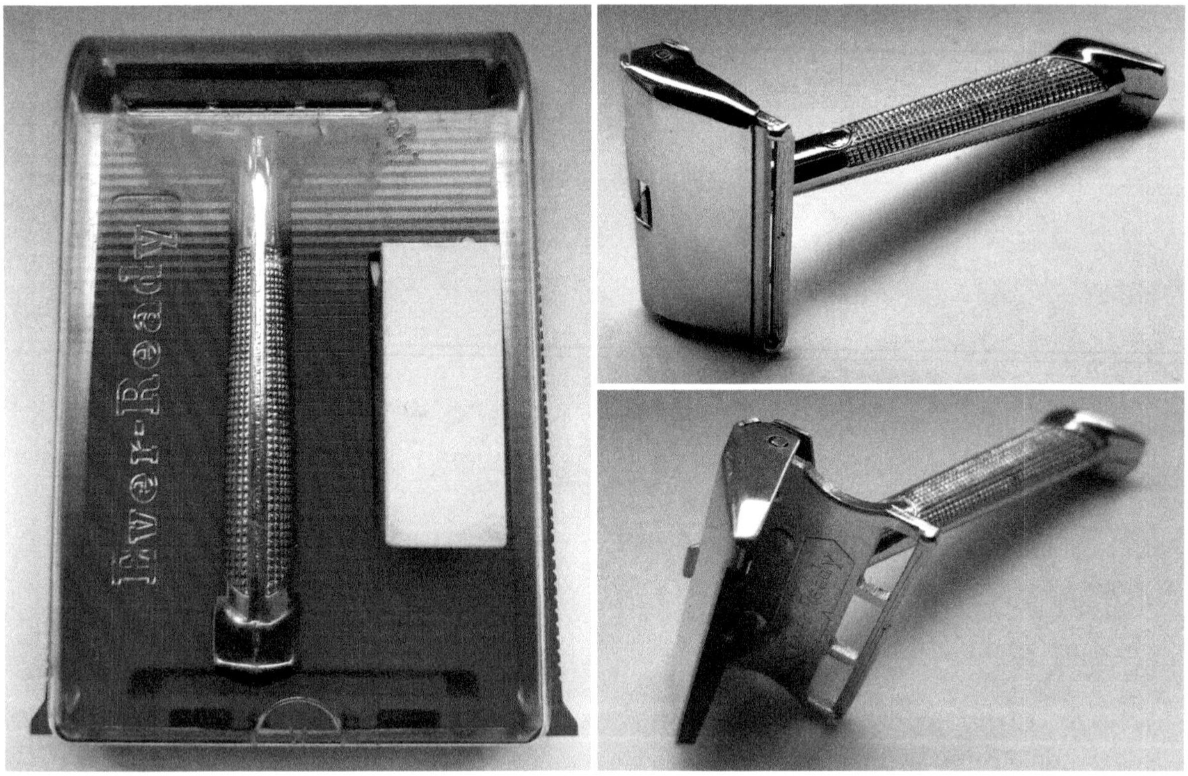

A vintage Ever-Ready 'E Bar' SE razor, made in Great Britain.

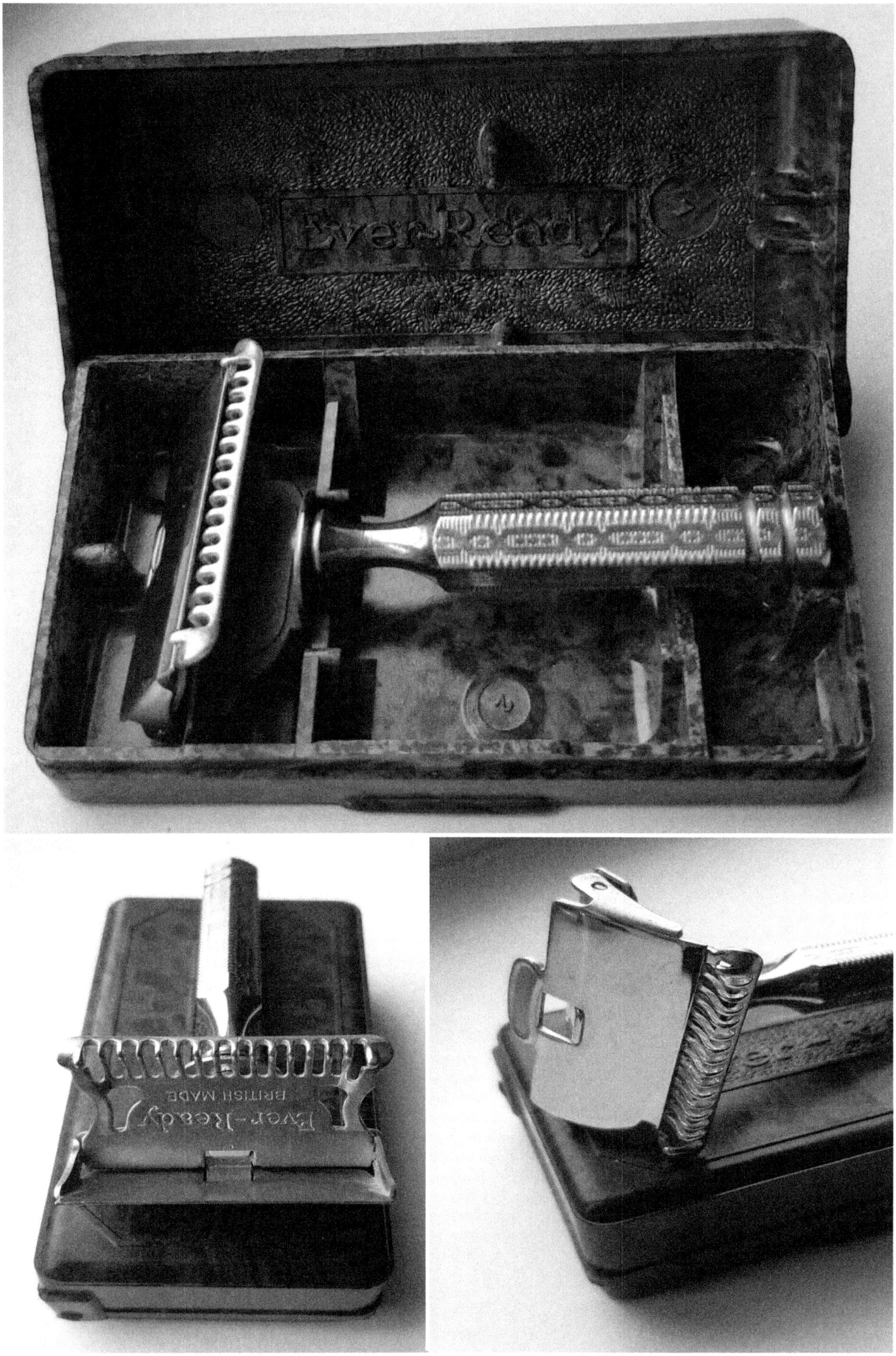

An Ever-Ready '1912' SE razor, complete with green bakelite box.

Adjustable Razors

Adjustable Razor Anatomy

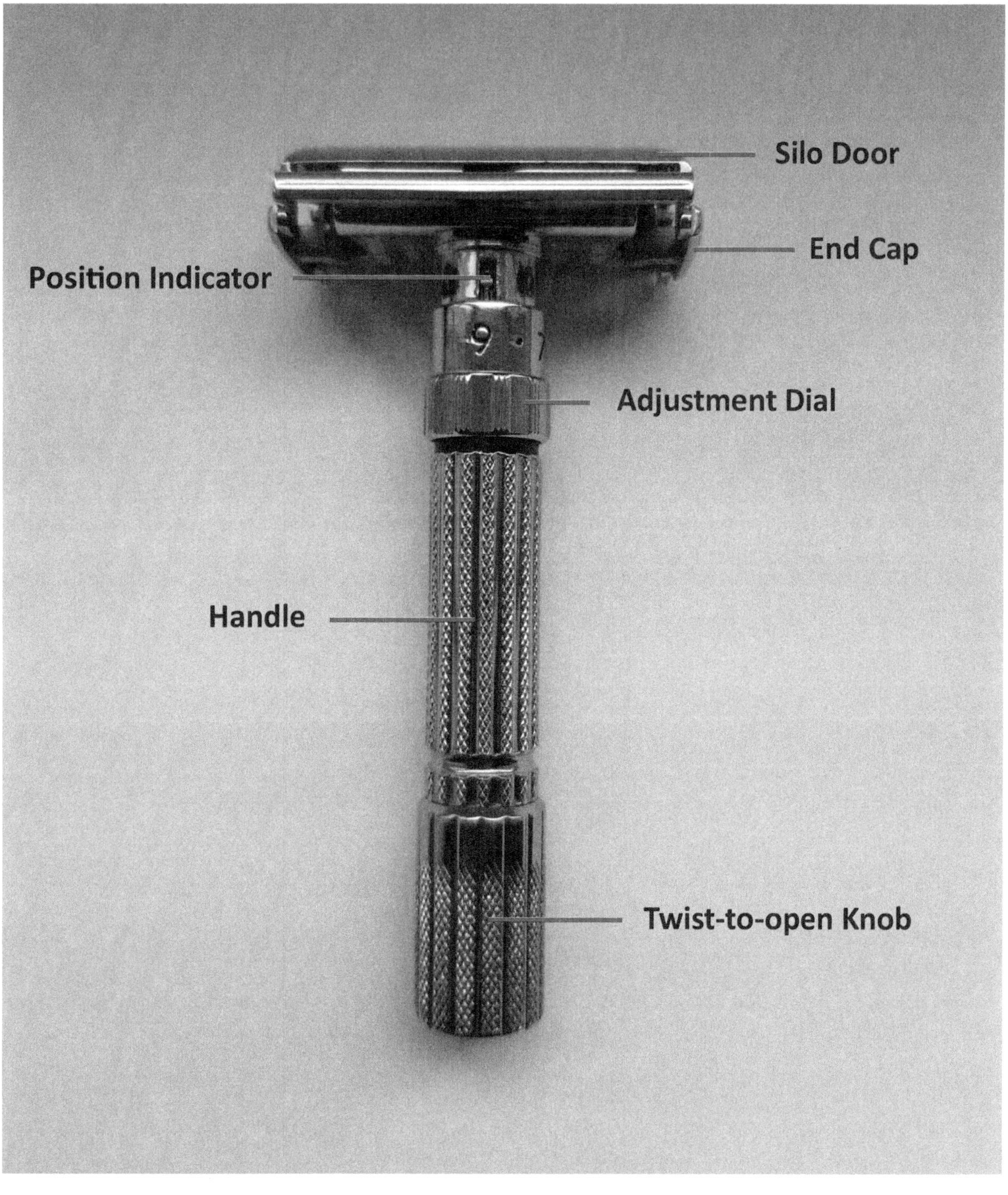

A 1959 (E4) Gillette 'Fatboy' nickel-plated adjustable razor which is a must for every vintage safety razor collector. Orginally known as the '$1.95', it became popularly known as the 'Fatboy' after the introduction of the Slim Adjustable razor in 1961. Gillette used stamp codes for their razors so that they could monitor sales in different parts of the country. E = 1959, 4 = 4th quarter of 1959.

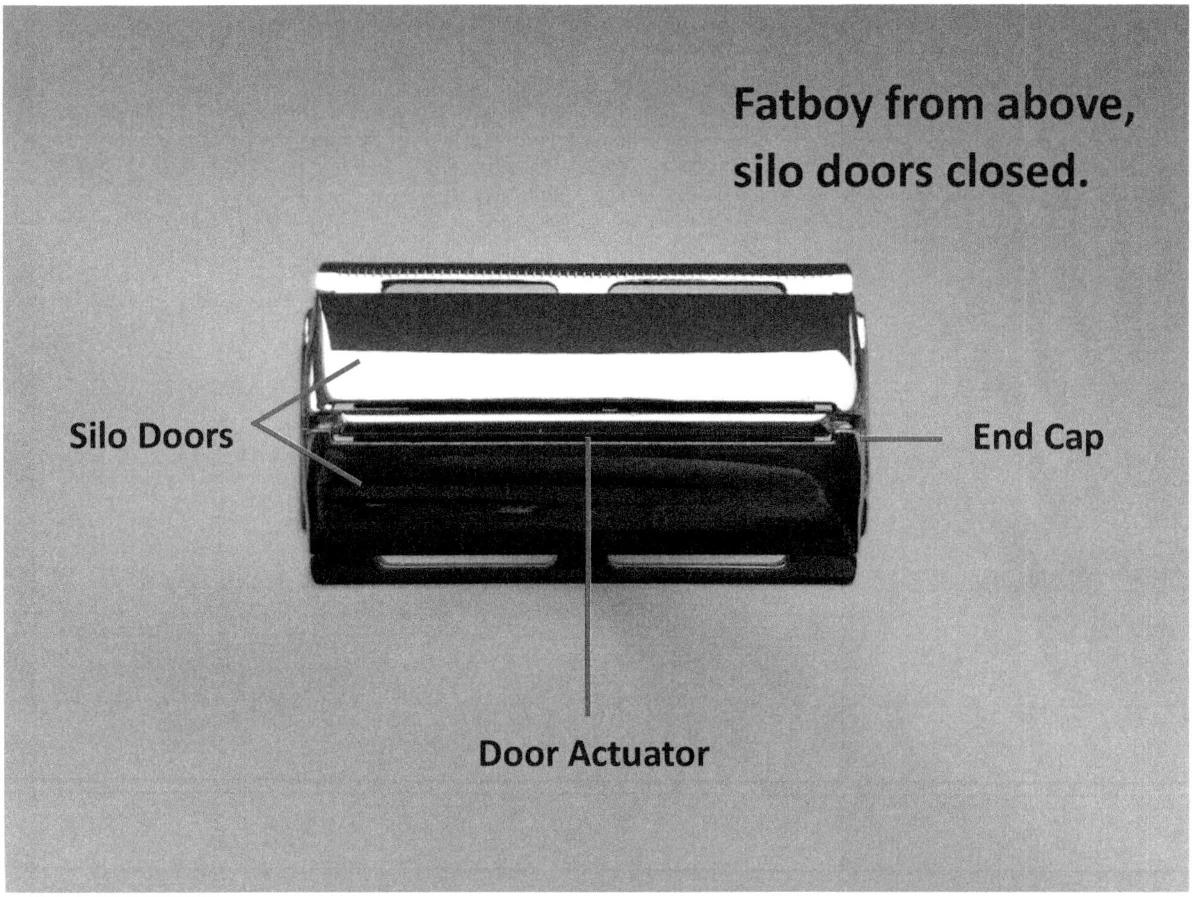
Fatboy from above,
silo doors closed.
Silo Doors
End Cap
Door Actuator

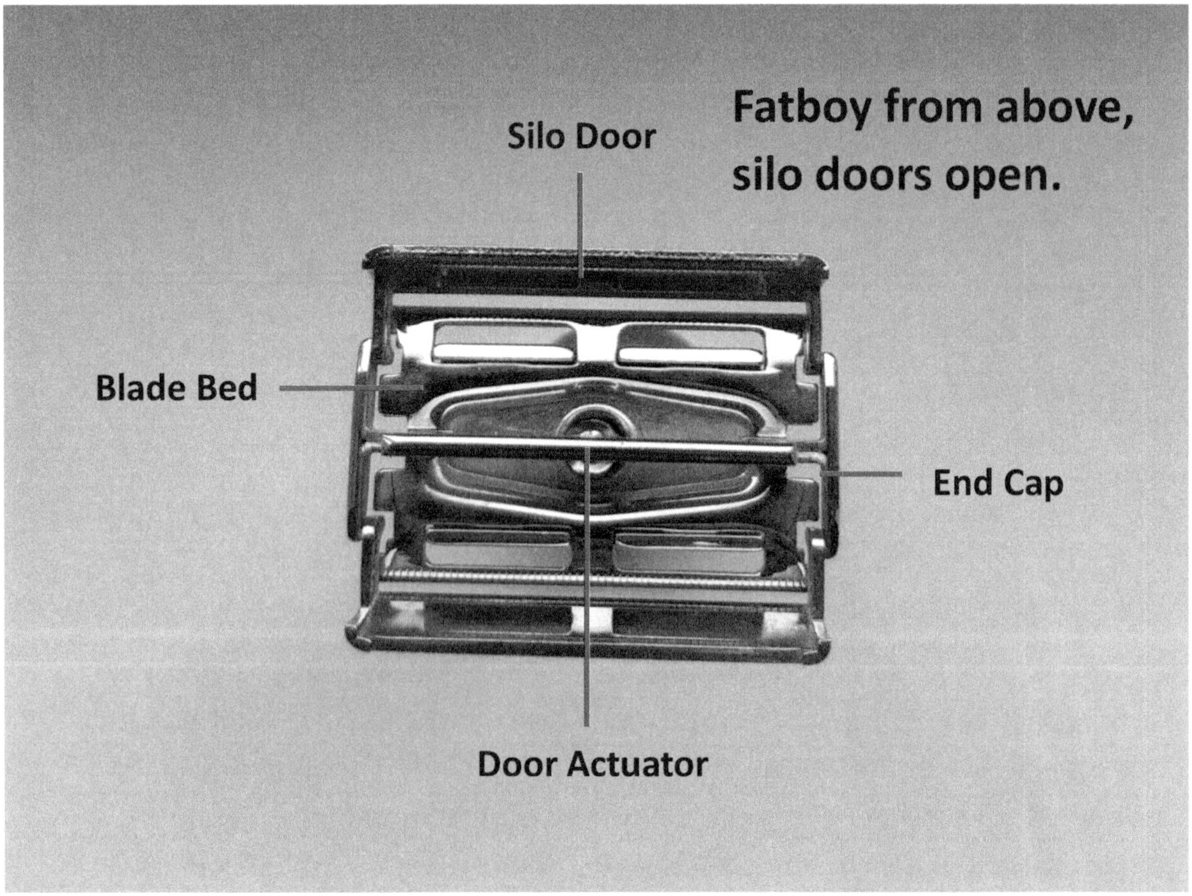
Fatboy from above,
silo doors open.
Silo Door
Blade Bed
End Cap
Door Actuator

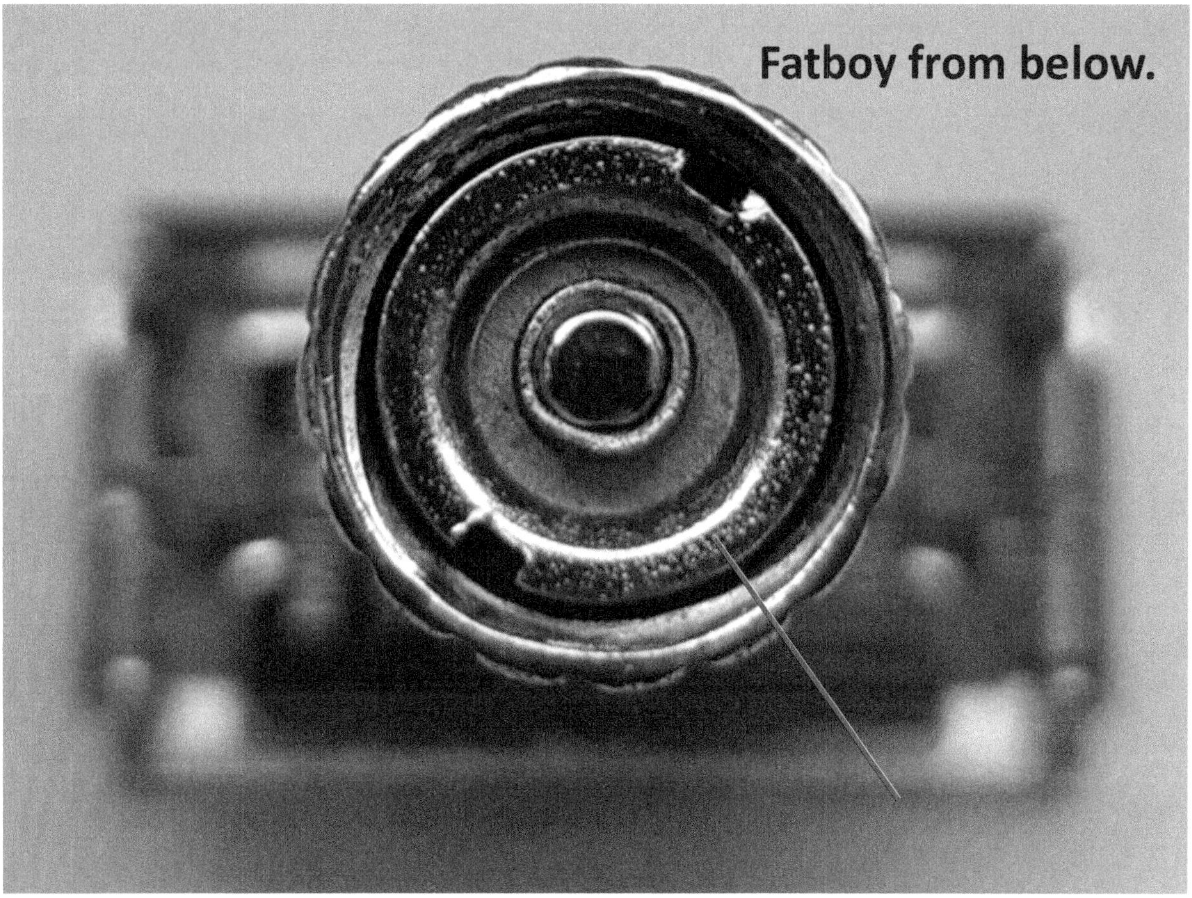

I don't advise anyone to disassemble Fatboy or Slim Adjustable razors unless they know exactly what they are doing. Instead, let an expert take care of any repairs or restoration work. As I write this book, I know of only one UK-owned business, JJ SHAVES, that specialises in DE razor cleaning, restoration and re-plating.

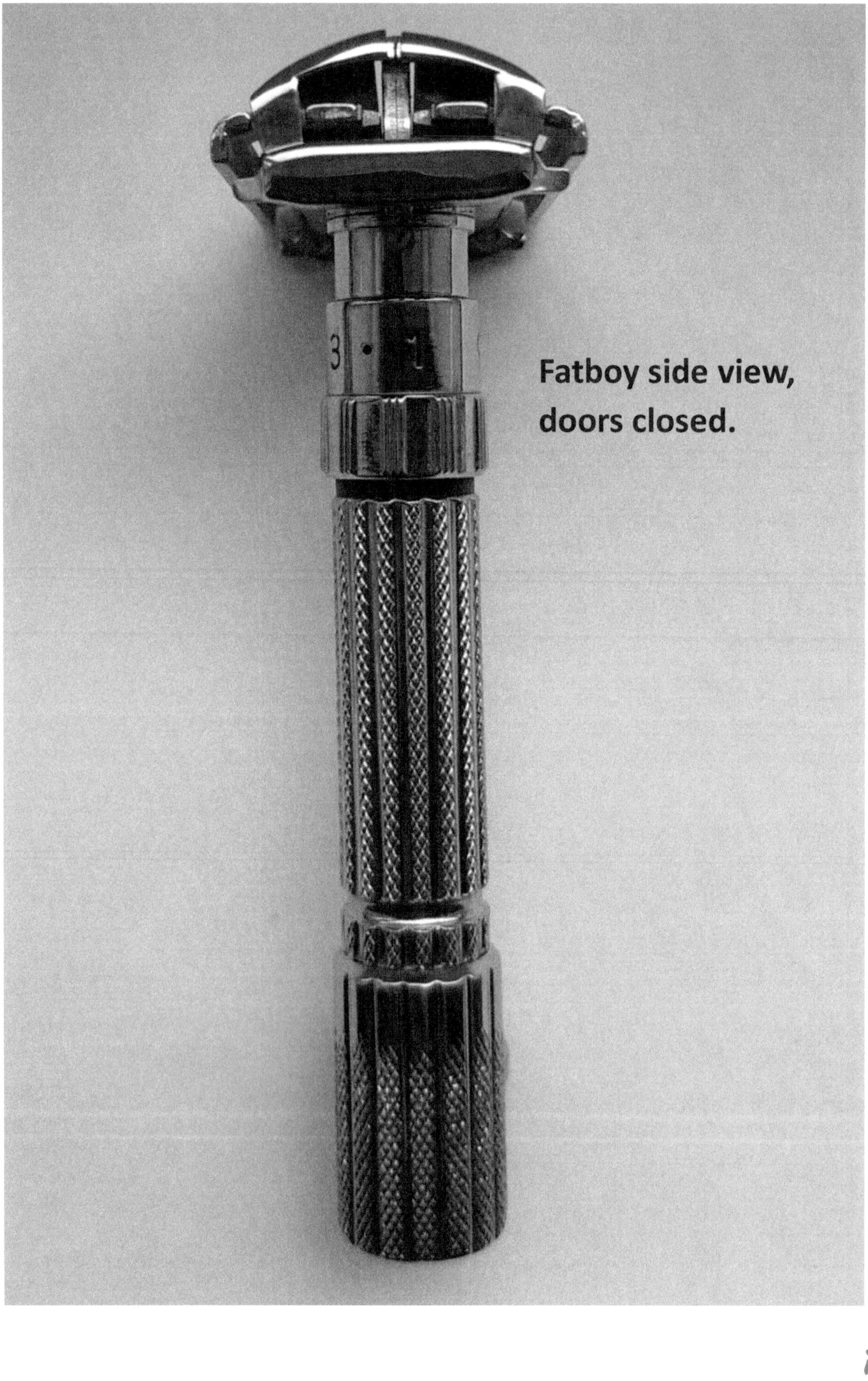

Fatboy side view, doors closed.

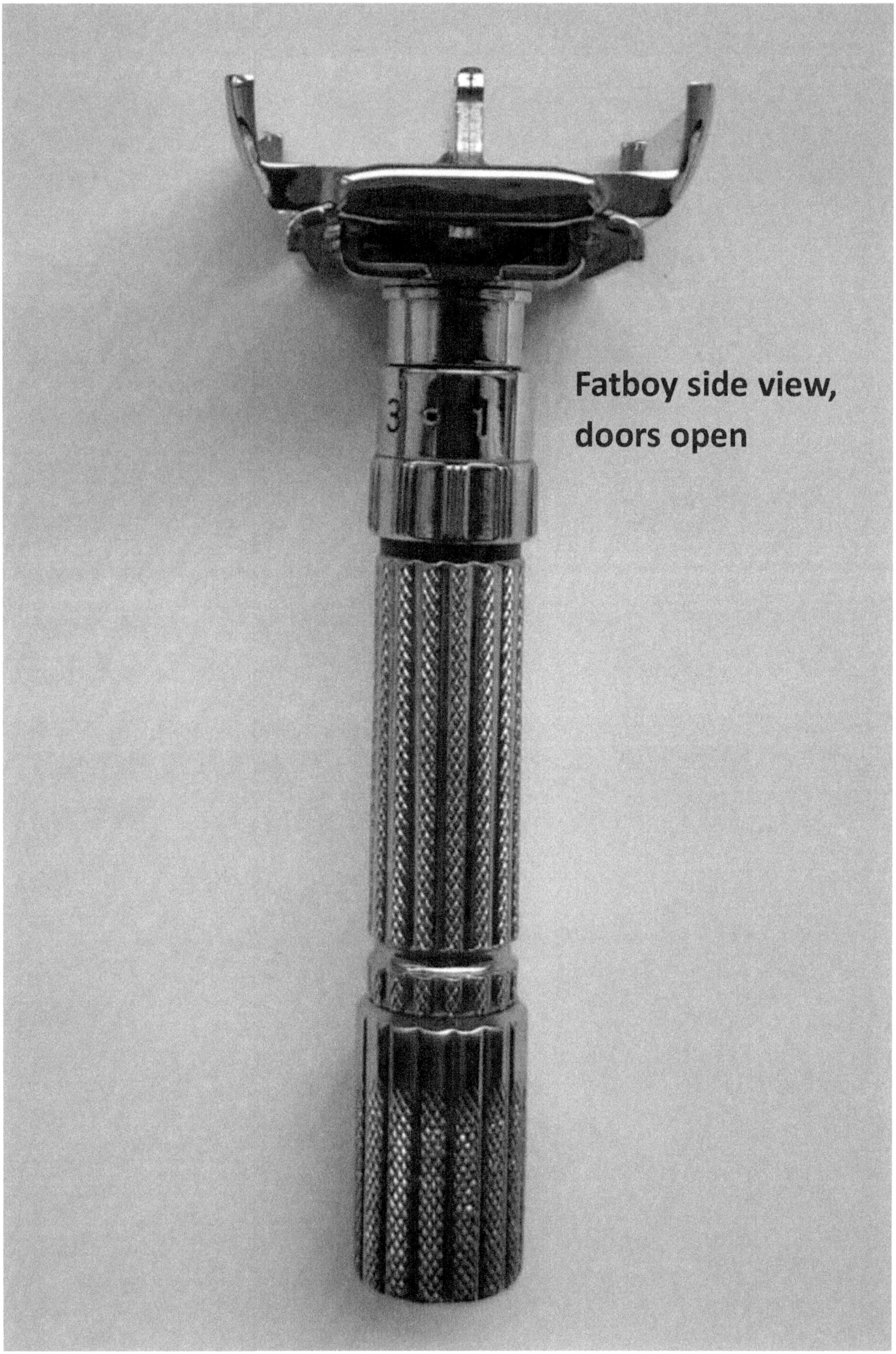

Fatboy side view, doors open

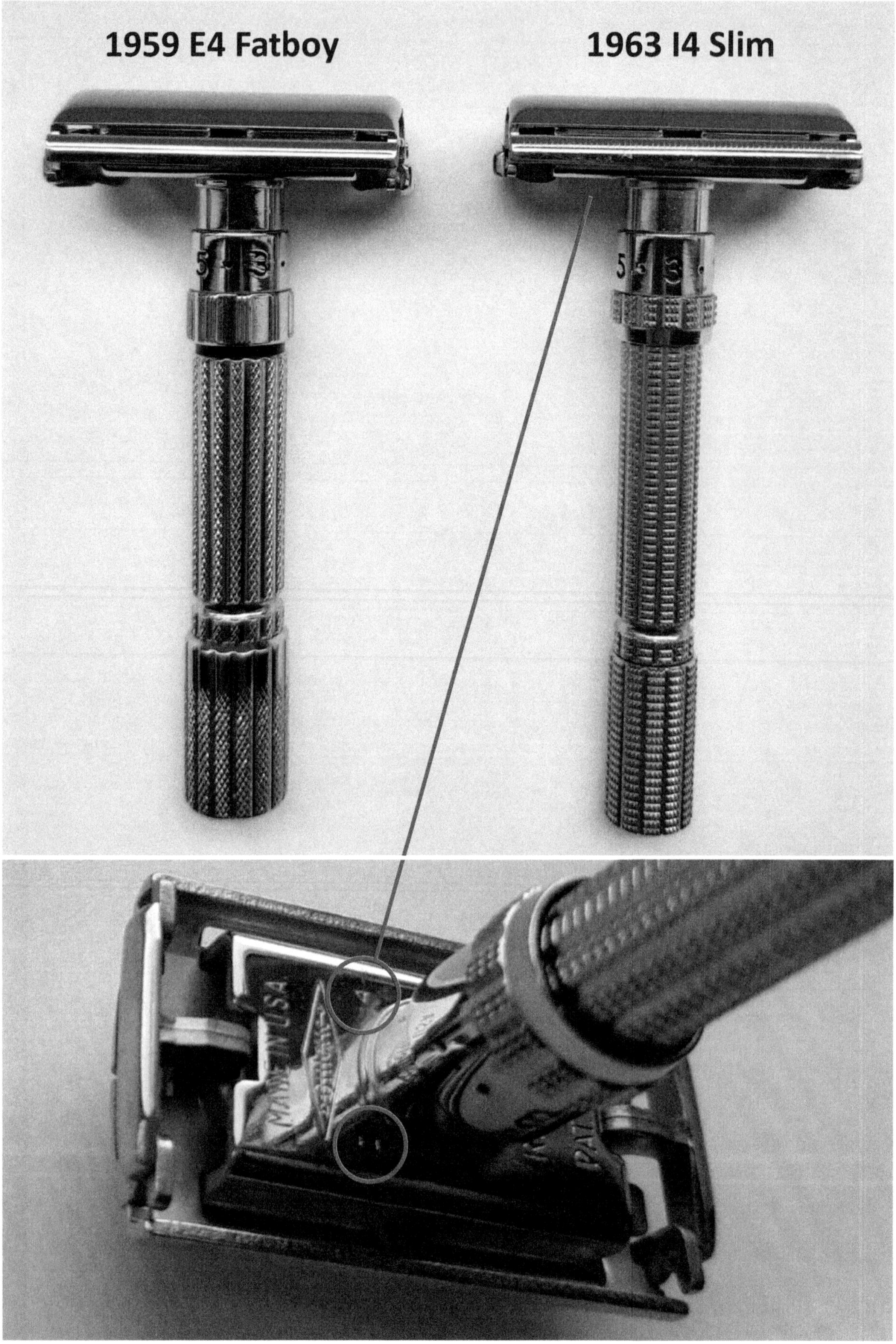
1959 E4 Fatboy
1963 I4 Slim

Butterfly Razors

Butterfly Razors

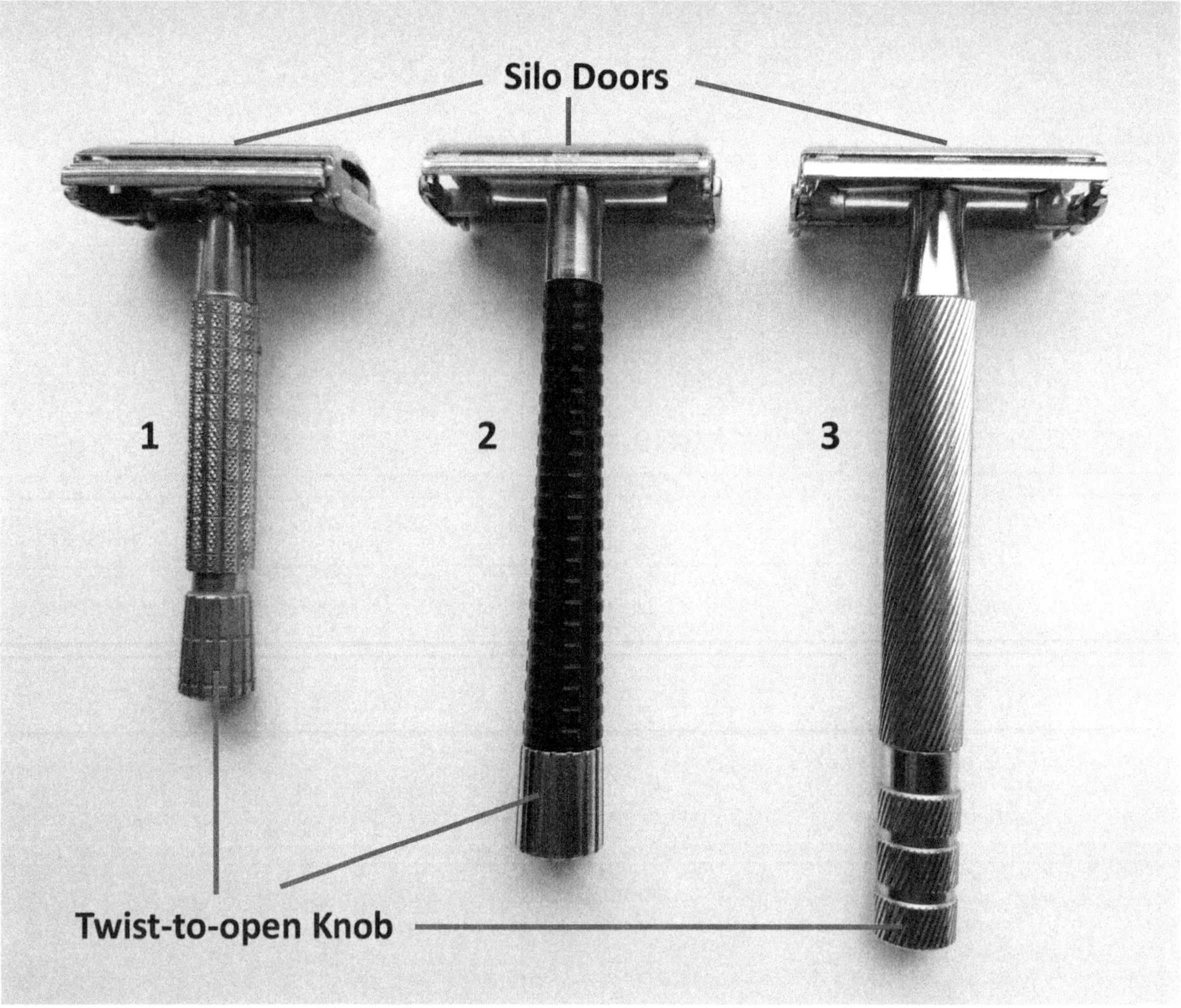

Butterfly razors are simply non-adjustable razors with silo doors that open and close by turning a knob at the end of the handle. Like all razors, some are more aggressive than others, so please bear that in mind if you decide to buy one. You'll have no control over the blade gap and will have to adjust your shaving technique accordingly i.e. the angle at which you press the blade to your skin.

1. **Vintage Gillette Flare Tip**
2. **Vintage gold plated Schick**
3. **Modern Wilkinson Sword Classic***

* The Wilkinson Sword Classic is available in some supermarkets in the UK and can be bought brand new on the internet. It comes with 5 blades.

Shavettes and Blades

Shavette SE Razor Blades

I don't and won't give advice on shavettes because to do so wouldn't be fair on you. I've tried using one on a number of occasions but just can't get along with it. If you are curious and want to learn more about shavettes, you would do better to watch some YouTube videos on the subject. There are many shavers on there who are more than proficient in the use of shavettes, so I'll leave the ball in their court.

Briefly, shavettes are those razors that barbers use when you go for a wet shave and/or neck and sideburn tidy-up. Barbers use them these days because they are not allowed to use their own straight razors by law for the simple matter of hygiene. However, if you own a well-honed straight razor, you can ask your barber to use it on you; a few straight razor enthusiasts that I've met indeed do this. Obviously, it is at the discretion of the barber, so please don't be disappointed if he tells you, with a worried look on his face, "thanks, but no thanks."

A shavette can be loaded with a snapped in-half-double edge blade but be very careful and always snap it while it is still in its wrapper.

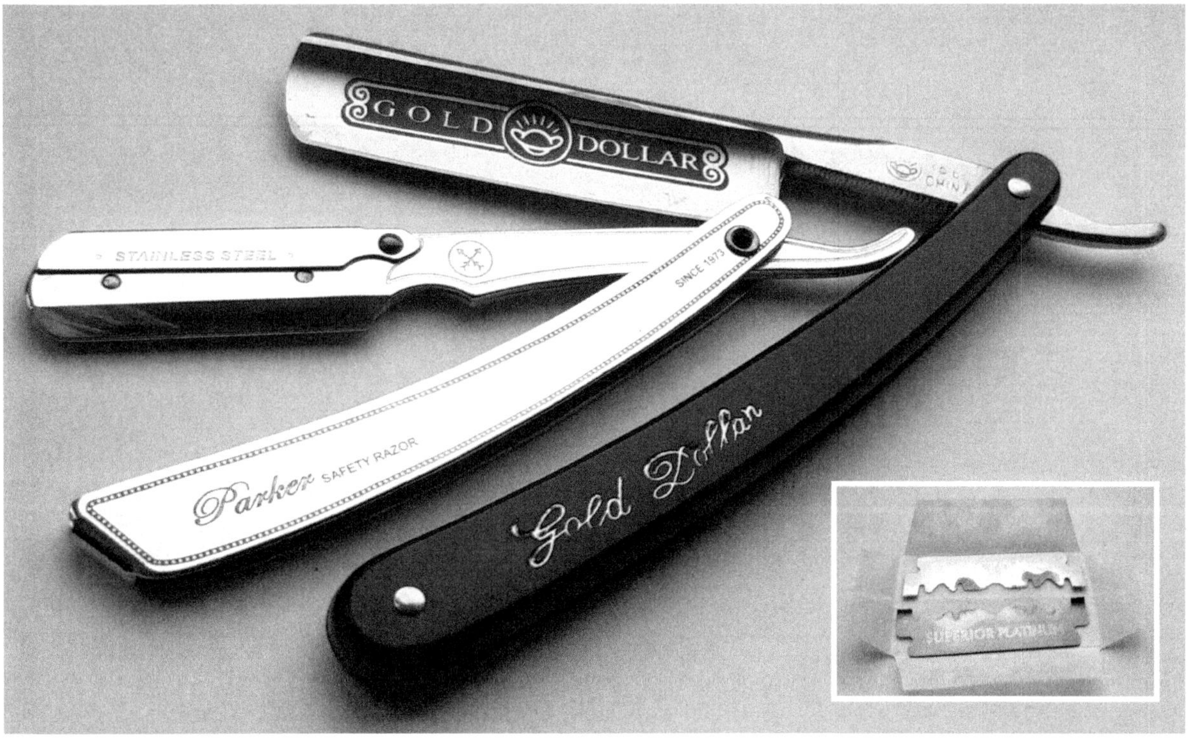

A Shavette being 'eaten' by a straight razor. Inset: A snapped DE blade.

Brushes

Anatomy of a Shaving Brush

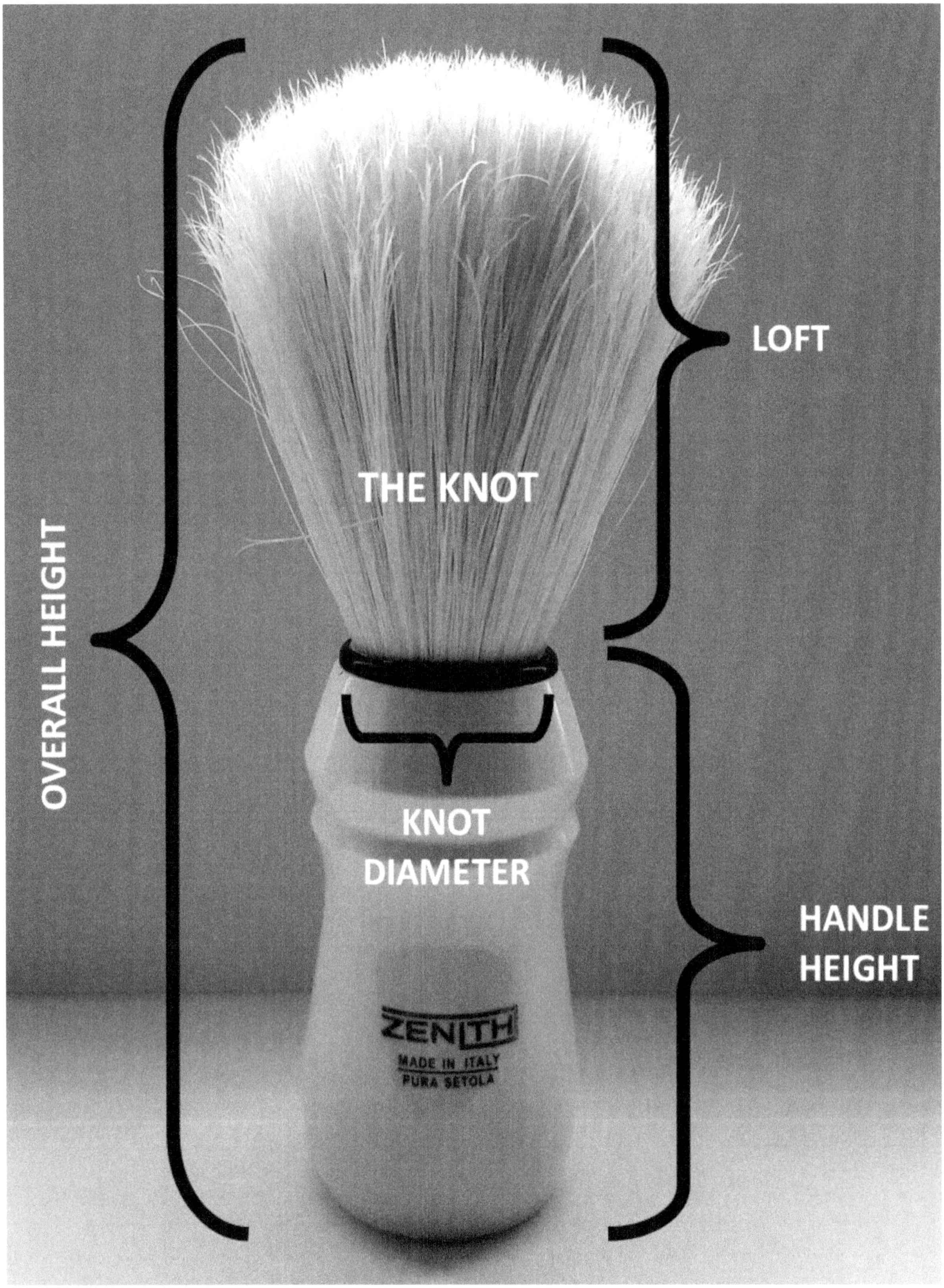

Shaving Brush Terms

Most traditional wet shavers prefer to use a shaving brush when ever they can for all number of reasons. I've listed the most common and obvious ones in the following tables. However, newbies to this kind of shaving need to learn and understand the terms so that they can make the right decisions about what sort of brush(es) they think would suit them and why.

Breaking-in

This applies to all brush types except synthetic. Boar bristles and horse hairs need to split in order to make them more soft and effective. Breaking-in a new brush is very important and newbies are often put off by their first attempt to create a satisfying lather from a brush straight out of its packet.

Exfoliation

A good shaving brush will help to prepare the skin by ridding it of dead skin cells and providing a smoother shave. Having said that, you should always clean your face well, preferably with a facial wash, before you start your shave. The best time for a shave is straight after a shower.

Backbone

This term describes how much resistance the brush gives when pressed into the skin. Invariably, a boar brush has more backbone than a synthetic, horse or most types of badger. Horse hair brushes, unless mixed with boar bristle, are actually quite floppy when wet, depending on what proportion of the hair is from the mane or tail of the horse.

Animal Smell

Many new animal brushes, particularly the cheaper variety, smell strongly of the animal they came from. The smell will disappear in time during the breaking-in process, so please don't be put off straight away.

SYNTHETIC

Advantages	Disadvantages
No breaking-in	Poor exfoliation
Very soft	Non-biodegradable
Sensitive skin friendly	

BOAR

Advantages	Disadvantages
Inexpensive	Breaking-in required
Very good exfoliation	Animal smell (in some cases)
Ethical*	Detrimental to sensitive skin (in some cases)

HORSE

Advantages	Disadvantages
Inexpensive	Breaking-in required
Ethical*	Animal smell (in some cases)
	Weak backbone (floppy)
	Detrimental to sensitive skin (in some cases)

HORSE/BOAR MIX

Advantages	Disadvantages
Inexpensive	Breaking-in required
Stronger backbone than horse	Animal smell (in some cases)
Ethical*	Detrimental to sensitive skin (in some cases)

BADGER

Advantages	Disadvantages
Expensive	No Breaking-in
Visually appealing	Animal smell (in some cases)
Unethical**	Detrimental to sensitive skin (in some cases)

***Ethical:** Boar bristle is a by-product of slaughter for meat and other parts of the animal. In the case of horse, the hair is obtained from the mane and tail during grooming without harming the animal in any way whatsoever.

****Unethical:** Badgers are taken from the wild, kept in cages and slaughtered inhumanely, usually by clubbing with anything that comes to hand.

Author's note on badger brushes:

I do not own, and never will own, a badger brush. For that reason alone, I'm unable to provide photographs of badger brushes in this publication.

An increasing amount of shaving supply companies these days are now refusing to sell badger brushes for ethical reasons. Good quality synthetics are just as good, if not better, than badger brushes.

Only ethical brushes will be discussed in this book.

Breaking-in a Boar or Horse Brush

Congratulations! You've just bought your first boar, horse, boar/horse mix brush and want to use it straight from the packet. The only trouble is, you won't be able to use it straight away. When I say that you won't be able to use it straight away, I don't mean that there's a law against it and that the 'Shaving Brush Police' will come knocking at your door if you do. If you've never used an animal shaving brush before, you're going to have to wait at least 3-days to a week before it's ready for that first shave.

As I've already said, animal brushes have to be broken-in before they can be used. Some brushes need more breaking-in than others and a lot depends on the quality of the brush. Put simply, the cheaper the brush, the more breaking-in is going to be required to soften and split the hairs.

Let's not forget the fact that the brush is likely to smell of the animal it came from. You might sniff your first brush straight out of the packet and think it doesn't smell much of anything. If this is the case, run the brush under a warm tap for about 30 seconds and then have sniff of the whiff.

The warm water will release the aroma and again, depending on the quality of the brush, it's very likely that it's going to smell pretty funky. When I say 'funky', I don't mean in the James Brown sense.

Press the brush against the palm of your hand swirl it round. Chances are it's going to feel very stiff and scratchy. This is entirely normal, so don't throw it in the bin and reach for that handy shaving foam in a can just yet. Just like a wild stallion, your brush has got to be broken-in so that it serves you well for years to come.

The bristles have to be made to split at the ends in order for them to soften. In turn, this will enable them to create a better lather and hold substantially more of it.

Some 'macho' shavers just get on with it and put up with poor lather and smelly brushes by breaking them in as they go. Fine, but if you want to break-in your brush before you use it, the following pages explain how. All you need is a glass, comb, shampoo/conditioner and rough towel.

A boar brush straight out of its packet. Notice how straight the bristles are before the breaking-in process. The razor blade is for size comparison only.

Above: These are some of the steps taken to break-in a brush and will be explained further on the next page.

BREAKING-IN PROCESS

Repeat the following process for 3-7 days and you will be left with a sweet smelling, shave-ready brush.

- Run the brush under a warm tap until it is soaked through.
- Apply some shampoo and rub into the bristles thoroughly for a couple of minutes or until you get bored. To get a better, quicker result, use a shampoo with conditioner or condition after shampooing.
- Leave the brush to stand for 1-hour without rinsing it.
- Rinse thoroughly, again under warm running tap water. Never expose the brush to scalding hot water and under no circumstances soak it in freshly boiled water because the glue holding the knot will melt and you'll end up with a handle without any bristles.
- Flick the brush in the air to rid it of excess water.
- Rub the brush on a towel. The rougher the towel, the better. Use an old towel for this, not one that's already hanging in the bathroom because your family won't appreciate drying their hands on a towel that smells like a wet hog. Boar brushes actually like a bit of rough towel treatment when they are being broken-in, so give yours a good swirling up, down, side to side, round and round. If you've completed the shampoo stage properly and allowed the conditioner to soak in, the bristles should be soft and pliable enough not to snap.
- Wash and dry the towel ready for the next day.
- You might find that the odd bristle comes loose. Don't panic because this is perfectly normal. You're just getting rid of odd bristles that would have fallen out anyway. This is another good reason to break-in a brush before using it; it's better to lose the odd bristle on the rough towel than on your face during the lathering. Having said that, all brushes lose the odd bristle or hair over time but the rate at which this happens can be slowed and I'll explain about that in the section about caring for your brushes.

- Put the brush into a glass of cold water. Don't soak the base of the knot if you can help it. Keep the level of the water just below it.
- Place the glass containing the brush on a shelf at the back of the fridge and leave for 24-hours. Let family members know that it's there so they don't knock it over looking for a midnight snack.
- Remove the glass from the fridge and the brush from the glass. You might notice that the water level has dropped. This is because the bristles have soaked up some of it. Make sure you replace the stale water with fresh at each further stage.
- Rinse the brush thoroughly under warm running water and give it a sniff. Don't be surprised if it still smells of animal because it's still early days.
- Flick the brush dry and rub it on a clean towel using the same method as before. Don't be afraid to give it a good scrub.
- Now it is time to apply a comb to the brush in order to split more bristles and tease out any loose ones. Grip the base of the knot tightly between the finger and thumb of one hand and comb the brush away from the knot with the other hand. Use the broad teeth of the comb to begin with and then finish off by using the fine teeth.

Hold the base of the knot firmly; you only want to get rid of the loose bristles. Use the broad end of the comb first, followed by the fine.

The boar brush after 7-days of the breaking-in process. It no longer smells of wet hog and the bristles have started to split. The brush is now ready to use and its performance will improve over time. With regular use, the bristles split further and hold more lather. If looked after properly, the brush will last for years.

An example of a boar/horse mix brush before undergoing the breaking-in process. The bristles are very upright but it must be said that a boar/horse brush mix is somewhat softer to start with than a pure boar bristle brush.

The exact same brush after 7-days of breaking-in. The bristles are splitting and smell sweeter now the process is complete. The brush will become more efficient the more it is used and properly looked after. Inset: View from above.

Looking After Your Brush

Look after your brush and your brush will look after you, so taking care of a brush will increase its life by many years and keep it smelling clean and fresh. If you leave a damp brush standing on the bathroom shelf it will go mouldy, smell unpleasant and eventually the bristles will start falling out.

Rinse it

After your shave, always rinse your brush under warm running water until no lather remains. Ensure that you run the water right into the brush down to the base of the knot and use your fingers to tease away any soap residue to prevent it turning scummy.

Dry it

Flick the brush in the air to remove as much water as you possibly can. Once done, rub it from side to side on a clean towel. If you're using a boar brush, the bristles will have soaked up a lot of water, especially if it's well broken-in with lots of lovely split bristles.

Hang it upside down

As I've already said, never leave a brush to stand upright until it is completely dry. Purchase a stand for this purpose. I have several stands because my brushes vary in size. Make sure you check the dimensions of the stand before you buy it.

Store it in a dry place

When it is dry, and I mean bone-dry, you can then stand the brush upright. If you have only the one brush and use it daily, it will never completely dry. On the other hand, if you are already down the Rabbit Hole, you can bet your bottom dollar that you will end up with a collection of different brushes of all shapes and sizes. I store my dry brushes in a cabinet away from the bathroom. Never store your brushes in the bathroom because the damp air will do it no favours whatsoever.

The correct way to dry your brush. Never feel tempted to leave a damp brush standing upright on the bathroom shelf, or any shelf, for that matter. Buy 2 or 3 stands of varying sizes if you own more than one brush. A brush may only be stood upright once the knot is completely dry. Don't keep brushes in the bathroom because damp will set in. Instead, store them away in a cupboard.

Mugs, Bowls and Cups

Mugs, Bowls and Cups

Shaving mugs and bowls can be bought specifically for the job. Alternatively, any old common or garden mug that you find at the back of the cupboard will do just as good a job. I mostly use an old mug that was originally intended for soup. It's wide, has a sturdy handle and holds a substantial amount of lather.

I own a couple of 'proper' shaving mugs, one of which (handmade by a company called 'Thrown In Stone') can be filled with hot water to keep a resting brush warm. However, I don't regard it as a true scuttle because it lacks steam holes, but opinions regarding this matter will and do differ. Incorporated into the bowl are circular ridges which work with the brush to create a very slick, creamy and sustainable lather.

The author's 'Thrown In Stone' shaving mug/scuttle.

The author's Shulton Glass 'Old Spice' shaving mug.

The only other custom vintage shaving mug that I own was made by Shulton Glass and would have contained Old Spice shaving soap when it was originally sold. It has vertical ridges to help with the lathering process.

Shulton Glass 'Old Spice' mugs have become very sought after by vintage shaving collectors and enthusiasts from all over the world.

A stainless steel shaving cup which is ideal to take on holiday.

Stainless steel shaving cups are perfect travelling companions because they're cheap to buy, light to carry, unbreakable and easy to keep clean. I would only ever use a cup such as this when I'm on holiday but many wet shavers use them on a daily basis.

As in all aspects of traditional wet shaving, it's your choice at the start, middle and end of each day.

The author's soup bowl that has, for a long time now, been used as a shaving mug.

My favourite shaving mug isn't a shaving mug at all. It is, in fact, a soup mug that I stumbled across at a jumble sale some 10-years ago. I paid about 25p for it at the time, which proves that you don't have to spend loads of money on custom-made, fancy shaving bowls with brand names plastered all over the outside and ridges and swirls on the inside.

If you have some sparc money and want to treat yourself, that's great but, if you don't, a mug from the kitchen cupboard will do the job just as well.

Scuttles

Scuttles

The author's ever-growing collection of vintage Shaving Scuttles.

Scuttles are very handy pieces of equipment and I use one of my many vintage scuttles every time I shave. Not only are shaving scuttles extremely practical, they are at the same time very attractive and come in many shapes, sizes and designs.

Scuttles are not used to create a lather. Their actual purpose is twofold; to soak the brush and keep an already loaded brush warm and hydrated between passes. Once the brush has soaked sufficiently, the water is replaced with fresh, hot (never boiling) water. The loaded (with lather) brush is then rested on top of the scuttle.

Steam subsequently passes up through holes to hydrate the knot and ensure that it stays nice and warm (see pictures on the next page).

Soaps, Croaps, Creams and Shaving Sticks

Soaps, Croaps, Creams and Shaving Sticks

One of the nicest aspects of traditional wet shaving is trying out all the many different types of soaps, croaps, creams and shaving sticks. You'll soon know that you are truly stuck down the Rabbit Hole when you start buying more before your last lot has run out! After all, when you were using that horrible foamy stuff from a can, I doubt if you considered buying more before you actually needed to.

Soaps, croaps, creams, shaving sticks, aftershaves, balms and the amount you own, will soon determine whether or not you are down the Rabbit Hole with the rest of us traditional wet shaving enthusiasts.

Soap

Usually quite hard, a shaving soap needs plenty of water to get it on the way to creating a lather. Often, a soap will need to be 'bloomed' before it can be used. Blooming simply means adding some drops of water to the soap before leaving it to stand so that the water is absorbed. Very hard soaps will need to bloom for longer, usually overnight, so make sure you plan ahead. When you come to use the soap, excess water left on top of the soap can be utilised as a pre shave.

Croap

Halfway between a soap and a cream, croaps look and feel like glazing putty. Once again, blooming is sometimes necessary to get the most out of a croap.

Cream

Cream doesn't ever need to be bloomed. It can be used straight from its jar or tube and can be applied directly onto a brush and/or whiskers. It can also be spread evenly in a shaving bowl, ready to be lathered with a brush.

Shaving Soap Stick

A shaving stick can be rubbed straight onto a wet face or damp shaving brush. A brush isn't essential because you can use your fingers to create the lather by massaging the soap residue left by the stick into the whiskers.

Soap from a Tub

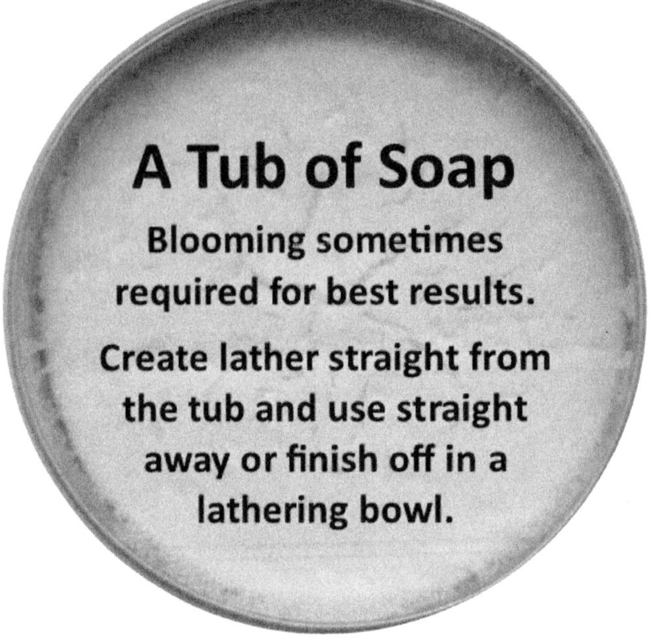

Cream from a Tub

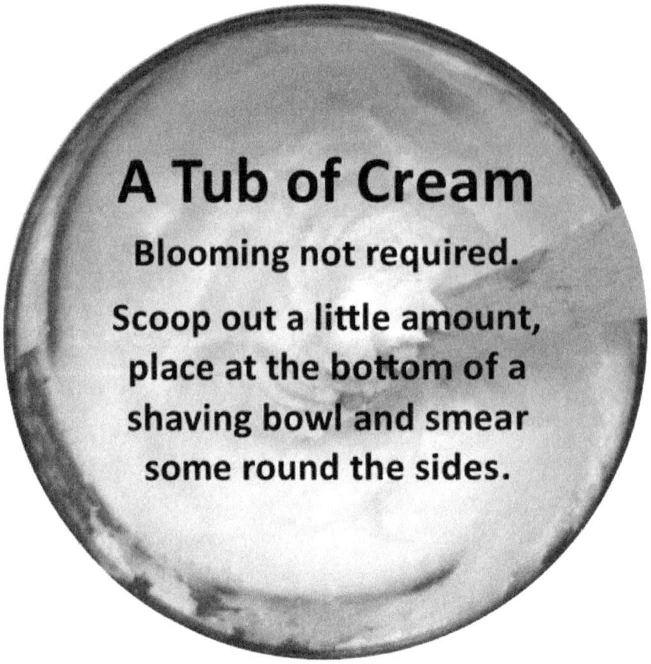

Croap from a Tub

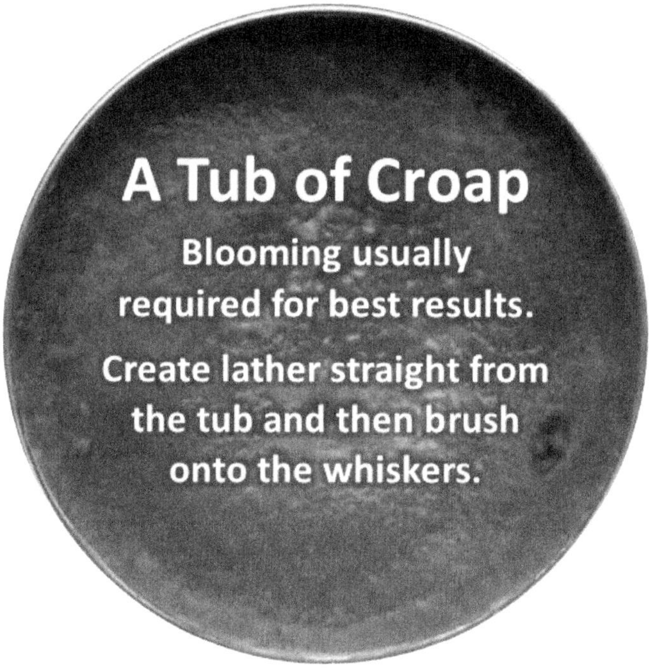

Cream from a Tube

Cream from a tube (above) can be massaged into the whiskers and a lather created with a damp shaving brush. Alternatively, if desired, the cream can be placed straight onto the shaving brush and lathered on the face.

Shaving Sticks

Shaving sticks are great little additions to any shaving den and they're what I take with me when I go on holiday. All you have to do is wet them, rub straight onto the whiskers and use your fingers to create a lather. Alternatively, you can apply a damp brush to the end and whip up a lather that way. Arko (above) is a very popular Turkish make of shaving soap and has a lovely aroma of fresh lemons. It's also sold in tubs.

Pre Shave Preparation

Pre Shave Preparation

Some shavers complain of having sensitive skin and suffering soreness after their daily shave. Many combat this problem by using products that are designed specifically for sensitive skin. Many traditional shavers, including myself, believe that multi-blade razors, poor quality shaving foam and general poor pre shave preparation is the mitigating factor when it comes to sensitive skin and soreness.

Good preparation is the key factor to achieving a good shave without soreness and rashes, so a shaving brush is seen by many as essential. Dragging a razor blade over poorly prepared skin is a recipe for trouble. After all, you wouldn't consider hanging paper on a dirty wall or painting over wood that you hadn't already washed and sandpapered, would you? Just like decorating your home, if you want a good result you have to put in all the necessary preparation beforehand. Any professional decorator worth his salt will tell you that preparation is the most important part of doing the job right.

Left: facial wash. Right: pre shave cream.

Splashing your face with warm water and smearing on cheap shaving foam straight out of a can will not do your face any favours if you genuinely believe or have been told by your doctor that you have sensitive skin.

Washing with a facial wash followed by a good rinse of clean water is the first, most important and often most overlooked step to successful shaving. For even more protection against soreness, a pre shave cream or lotion should be rubbed into the whiskers and left for a couple of minutes before lather is applied, ready for the first pass of the razor.

Aftershaves and Balms

Aftershaves and Balms

Aftershave not only smells nice, it also acts as an antiseptic for your freshly-shaved skin. Some are alcohol based and these are the ones that give you the 'burn'. Others are alcohol-free and vegetable extract based and contain only natural ingredients.

Again, it's entirely up to you to try different products and make up your own mind about which ones you like and which ones you don't like.

Aftershave is usually splashed on the face first and followed up with an application of balm. Balms help to cool the face, prevent soreness and rehydrate your skin after a shave.

Alternatively, you can forego the aftershave completely and go solely with a balm. There are many matching balms and aftershaves on the market but you can mix and match as much as you like. You might want to splash on a nice scented aftershave and follow it up with a neutral balm.

Whatever you decide, using aftershave and balm is one of the most enjoyable parts of wet shaving and it won't be long before you start receiving compliments about how nice you smell!

A matching set of aftershave and balm.

Bowl Lathering

Tub and Bowl Lathering

To bowl lather or not to bowl lather? That is the question. The answer depends on whether or not you enjoy it. I know quite a few traditional wet shavers who go out of their way to avoid it. Personally, I love to create lather in a bowl, whenever I can.

Sometimes, it's not possible to bowl lather. Some hard soaps and croaps are best lathered straight from their tubs, especially if they are the sort that need to be bloomed for a long time.

For instance, I tried on numerous occasions to bowl lather Mitchells Wool Fat soap but failed miserably every time. I blamed my hard tap water after reading that it can have an adverse effect on MWF.

Eventually, after admitting defeat, I asked for help on a shaving forum to find out where I was going wrong. It was pointed out to me that MWF has to be more or less soaked in water for at least a couple of days while still in its ceramic pot. I learnt that MWF (pictured) hates to be bowl lathered. I took heed of the advice, soaked the soap for a 3 days and then lathered straight from the pot. I was rewarded for my efforts with a brilliantly thick, slick and creamy lather. Ever since that day, I've made sure that I keep MWF very well-hydrated, even if I don't intend using it for days or many weeks at a time.

There's no shame in asking for help. There are many, many online shaving groups whose members are more than happy and willing to give advice on aspects of wet shaving. Never be afraid to ask because you will save yourself a lot of time and you might even make some new friends too.

Creating a Bowl Lather with Cream

Follow the steps in the table below and study the pictures on the next page to learn how to create a slick, rich lather using shaving cream and a brush. The more cream you put into your bowl, the more lather you're going to make. Creams vary in the amount of lather they produce, so start off with a blob about the size of a hazlenut.

Be very sparing with the water you add to the lather. You can put water in but you can't take it out. Too much water will kill the lather.

High end creams like those made by Taylor's of Old Bond Street (TOBS) are of such good quality that a small amount goes a very long way, so please bear this in mind if you don't want to waste any.

1	**If you are going to use an animal brush, soak it for 20-30 minutes in warm water, preferably in a scuttle. Synthetic brushes do not need to be soaked and can be held under warm running water for a minute or so.**
2	**Place a blob of cream about the size of a hazlenut in the bottom of the bowl. Using your finger, smear it evenly around the sides. I don't like getting my fingers messy, so I use an ice cream stick instead.**
3	**Take your brush and shake off any excess water. Avoid using a sopping wet brush because to much water will swamp the cream. Water will be added to the cream during the bowl lathering process, as and when required.**
4	**Hold the mug in one hand and the brush in the other. Put the brush into the bottom of the bowl and swirl the cream around both clockwise and anticlockwise. Do this until the interior of the mug is well coated.**
5	**Add just a few drops of water to the cream. If you are using a scuttle, you do this by dipping the end of the brush into the spout. If you are taking water straight from the tap, just wet your fingers and let a couple of drops of water fall into the bowl. Never put the bowl under the tap.**
6	**Continue swirling the lather round and round. Push the end of the knot into the lather after every 20 or so swirls. Keep monitoring it. If it becomes dry, again add a very little amount of water. Continue this process until you have a lather that you are happy with. Some people prefer thick lathers whilst others prefer thin. As with all things wet shaving, it's entirely up to you to decide.**

The lather is ready, the brush is loaded and resting on a vintage 1950s' James Kent Old Foley shaving scuttle. Water filled shaving scuttles are very useful pieces of equipment when it comes to bowl lathering. When more water is needed, the end of the brush can be dipped lightly into the spout 'for a drink'.

Mapping

Mapping Your Face and Whiskers

Mapping and learning about your face and whiskers is a very important skill that you'll have to master if you're seriously considering wet shaving in the traditional way.

Whiskers grow in all directions and are as unique to every shaver as their fingerprints. If you want to achieve a BBS (baby bum smooth) face, you'll first have to explore your face and neck to work out the direction that your whiskers are heading. You'll also have to determine which parts of your face and neck require more passes to rid them of that scratchy, annoying, leftover stubble.

I don't readily recommend that newbies attempt more than one pass when they start out down the Rabbit Hole. DE blades are a lot more effective than the 5-bladed plastic monsters that have become so popular in today's troubled world of shaving. One pass with the grain of the whiskers using a DE razor and blade is usually sufficient for a someone to go out into the world looking clean shaven and presentable. It's only as you get deeper down the Rabbit Hole that you will begin to strive for perfection. As we all know, perfection is only achieved by dedicated study, practise and making lots and lots of mistakes.

The best way to start mapping your face isn't by standing in the bathroom and staring at your whiskers to determine in which direction they are all growing. The very best way is to leave your whiskers to grow for a couple of days and use the back of your hand to do the exploring.

Rub the back of your hand over your face and neck to feel the direction of the growth. When you are moving against the grain of the whiskers it will feel a lot scratchier than when you move with the growth.

Take time to explore and make mental notes. Even better, draw some simple pictures like the one on the next page and mark the direction of the strongest growth with arrows.

This might sound silly but it's a very good way of mapping your face and developing muscle memory before you even pick up a razor. If you feel embarrassed, do it when nobody else is at home.

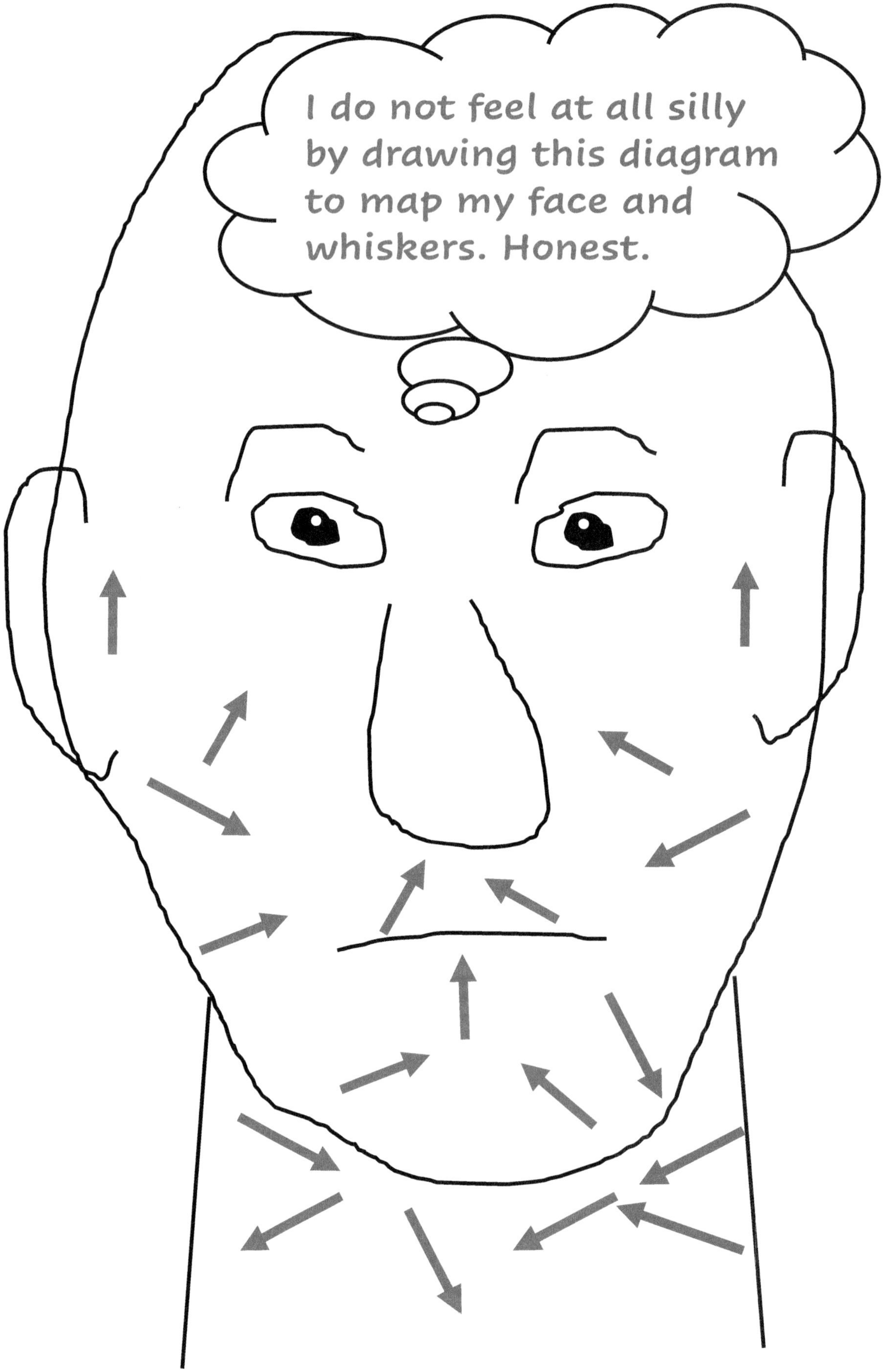
I do not feel at all silly by drawing this diagram to map my face and whiskers. Honest.

Weepers and Cuts

Dealing with Weepers and Cuts

Weepers and cuts are occupational hazards that every traditional wet shaver has to accept and learn how deal with. Fortunately, there are tools of the trade that can be utilised to stop minor bleeding and every wet shaver should have them to hand every time he applies a razor blade to his skin.

No one's facial skin is perfectly smooth. We all have bumpy bits, moles and scars. Some people are 'blessed' with cleft chins which can prove very tricky to shave. As I've already explained, preparation before a shave is absolutely paramount to achieving a good result and minimising soreness.

However, no matter how much preparation you put in, you *will* get the odd weeper and cut from time to time.

What is a weeper?

A weeper is a little spot of blood that appears as you shave or sometimes when you've finished shaving. Feeling all pleased with yourself having completed a shave, you look in the mirror and see tiny little specks of blood appearing before your eyes. Weepers don't run with blood because the abrasion is so small that the blood congeals almost immediately it meets the air. A weeper is the result of the razor blade taking off a thin layer of skin and this can happen easily if you shave over a pimple. Weepers can be treated effectively with the application of an alum block and will soon be forgotton about.

What is a cut?

A cut is somewhat different from a weeper and is a little more difficult to deal with. If you've cut yourself, you haven't just taken off a small layer of skin, you've sliced *through* the skin. Most shaving cuts can be dealt with by applying a dampened styptic pencil. However, if you sustain a cut so deep that it won't stop bleeding, it's time to visit the accident and emergency department of your hospital because you might need a stitch. Cuts only occur when you mishandle the razor or if the razor slips in your hand, causing the blade to move sideways instead of straight forward.

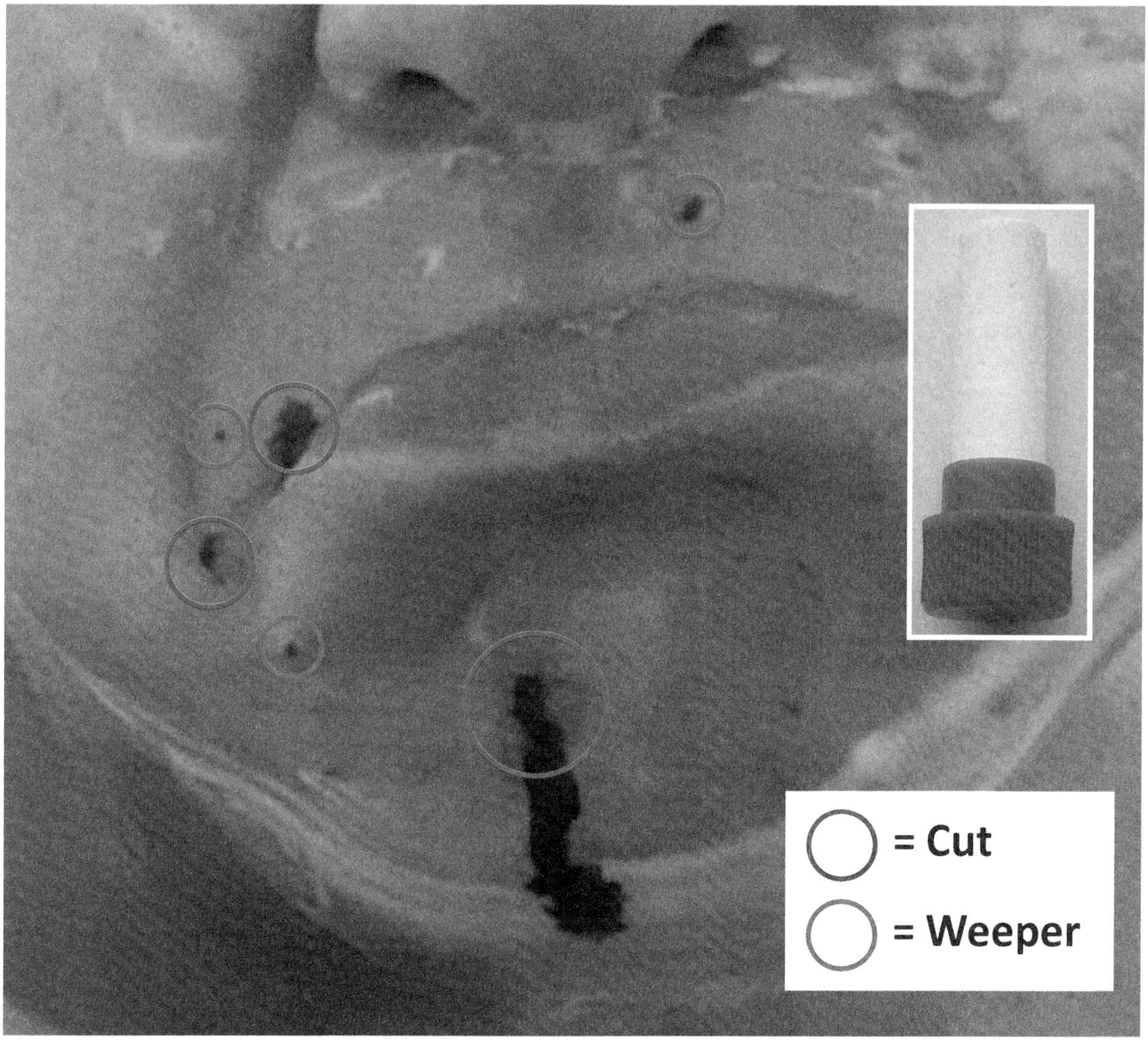

The poor chap in the picture (above) has an assortment of cuts and weepers that he'll have to deal with. Fortunately, he always keeps an alum block and styptic pencil to hand whenever he has a shave. He'll rub a damp alum block over the weepers and leave to dry. The cuts will need to be treated with a styptic pencil which he will dampen at the end and again, leave to dry. No stitches necessary.

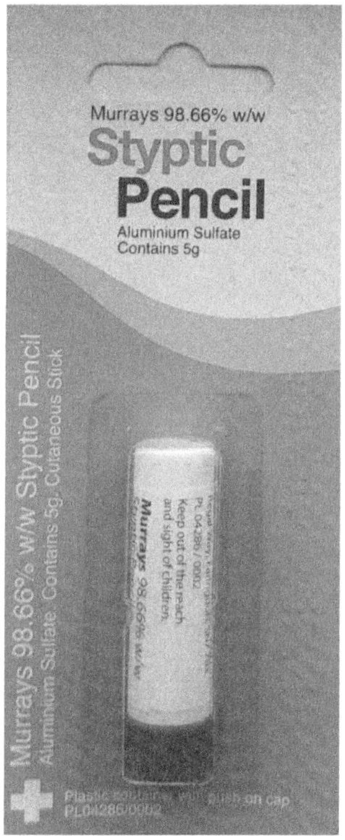

Left and above inset: Styptic pencil. Above: Alum block.

Passes

Passes

When wet shavers talk about 'passes', they are describing how many times they pass the razor over their face in a single shave. There are some enthusiasts who don't think that one pass is enough to get a BBS. Having said that, not everyone wants a BBS. Many shavers are quite happy with one pass in order to eradicate stubble .

As I've already said, I don't recommend newbies to attempt 3 passes on their very first shave. If you've been using disposable and/or cartridge razors for years, you will have adapted your muscle memory to pressing the razor hard against your face to get rid of the whiskers. If you apply the same technique with a DE or SE razor, you're going to end up with a very sore, if not cut, face. However, when you become more proficient with a DE or SE, you'll want to achieve that BBS.

The most popular 3-pass method:

1. **1st pass with the grain - straight down the face.**
2. **2nd pass across the grain - straight across the face.**
3. **3rd pass against the grain - straight up the face.**

The majority of wet shavers complete their shaves in the order listed. However, I prefer to shave against the grain on the second pass and across the grain on my third. I do this because it's the way I taught myself to shave when I was using the dreaded disposable razors, so it's what I'm used to and it's my preference.

If you have mapped your face properly, you'll know which direction your whiskers grow and only you can decide how to approach them with your razor. Experimentation is the key and the more you shave, the more you will learn about your whiskers' growth patterns.

The neck area has, usually, the most complicated of all growth patterns, so mapping it properly before you shave is extremely important.

1st pass
with the grain

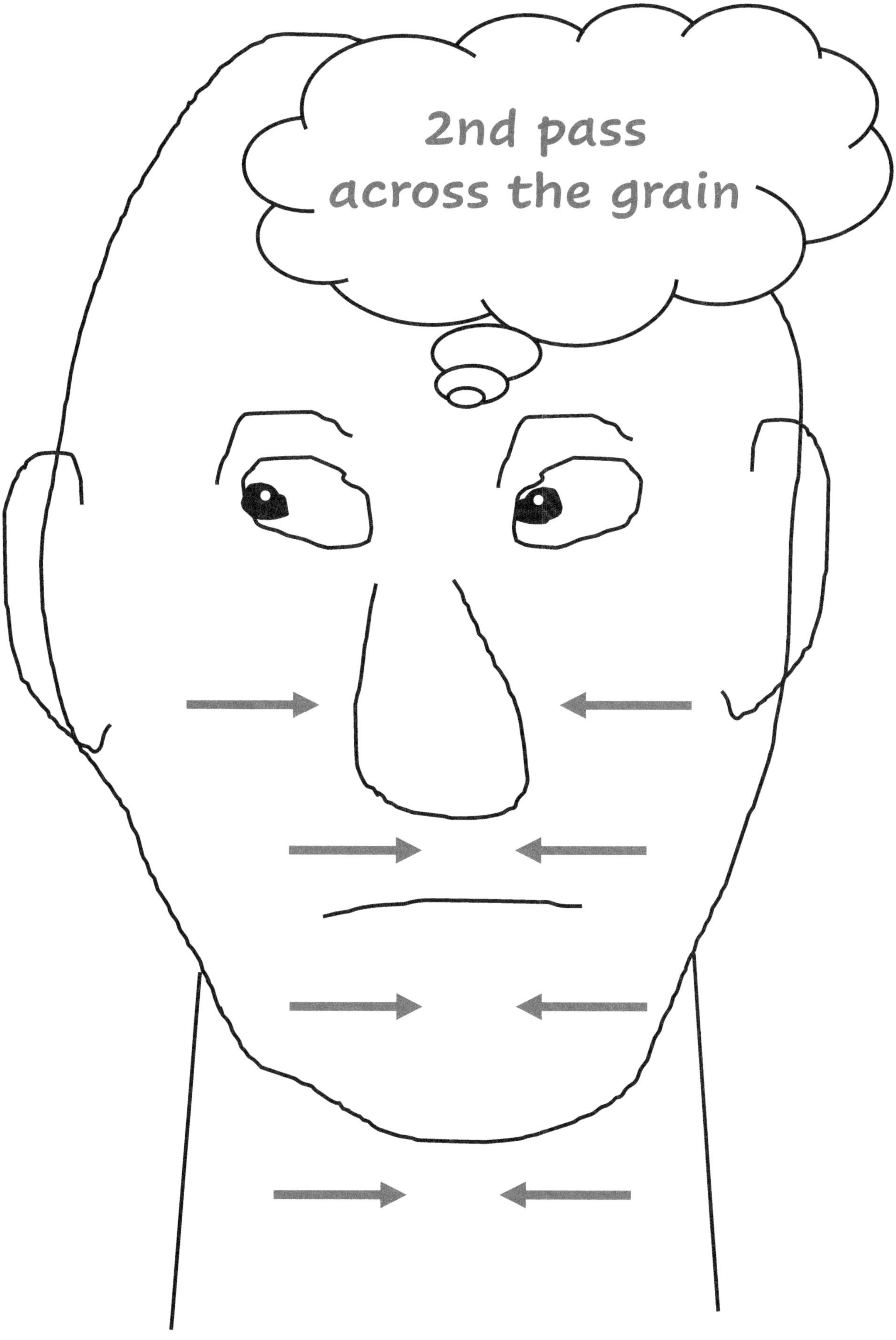
2nd pass
across the grain

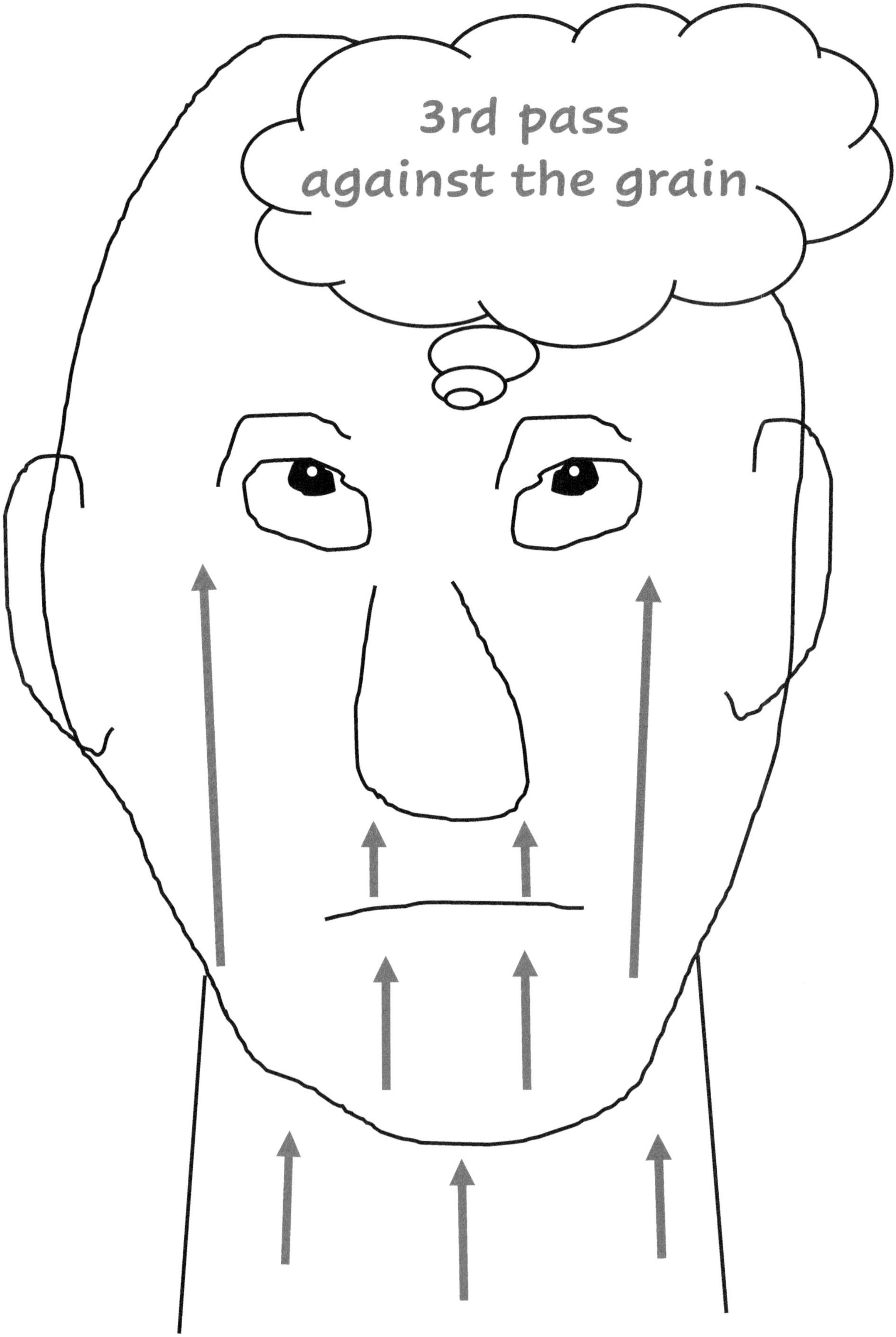
3rd pass
against the grain

First Shave and Shaving Steps

Your First Proper Shave

You are almost at the end of this book and, as you've come this far, you'll have learnt a lot about traditional wet shaving. It's now time for that first shave with your newly-acquired DE razor, so I'll pass the baton (sorry, razor) to you and hope that you enjoy yourself.

Don't forget, it isn't a race against time. You've got years to spend practising and perfecting your shaving techniques. Traditional wet shaving is about taking time to savour the experience, turning what was once a mundane chore into some quality time that is personal to you.

Set aside at least 20-minutes for a shave. Ask your family members if they want to use the bathroom before you start; there's nothing worse than being disturbed halfway through by someone who needs to use the toilet.

Start slowly and aim to complete one pass of the razor shaving *with* the grain. If you feel at any point that things are not going right, you can always stop and finish the shave with your cartridge, disposable or electric razor. Whatever you do, don't press as hard against your skin as you would with a disposable because you will cut yourself for sure. Put the cap of the razor flat against your face and slowly, very gently move it down your face a couple of inches at at time. If you feel comfortable with this and notice that you're not taking off any stubble, increase the angle *very* slightly. Enthusiasts' rule of thumb is that 30° is the optimum angle. All I can say is that I've never put a protractor to my face in order to measure the angle of a blade, so just use your common sense.

Also, use your ears. DE razors give good audio feedback, so you will be able to hear the whiskers being sliced off. It's one of the most satisfying aspects of shaving with a proper razor blade.

If you complete a full pass, reward yourself with a very well-deserved pat on the back, contemplate the next shave and think about the possibility of achieving 2 passes, the second being across the grain.

Good luck and welcome to the Rabbit Hole!

14 Shaving Steps

Follow the steps in the table below to achieve a single pass shave *with* the grain of the whiskers. I advise all newbies to complete a single pass without issues before attempting a second or a third.

However, if you feel confident after the first pass and your face and neck don't have any soreness, weepers or cuts, you might want to attempt a second pass *across* the grain followed by a third pass *against* the grain.

If you complete 3 passes, very well done. If you only manage half a pass, that's fine. You have the rest of your life to perfect your technique.

1	**Ensure that your alum block and styptic pencil are both close at hand, next to your bathroom basin or wherever you are whilst shaving.**
2	**Create the lather in a bowl. This won't be necessary if you are going to apply a shaving stick or a brushless shaving cream straight to your face and whiskers.**
3	**Wash your face with facial wash and rinse with warm water.**
4	**Rub pre-shave lotion well into the whiskers.**
5	**Use the brush to apply lather or rub on brushless shaving cream.**
6	**Put the razor cap flat against your skin.**
7	**Move the razor down a couple of inches and listen. Is there audio feedback? If there is, it means you are now removing whiskers from your face. If there is not, increase the angle *very* slightly and try again.**
8	**Once satisfied that you are using the razor correctly, shave the rest of your face and neck with the grain.**
9	**Rinse with warm water, look at and feel your face.**
10	**If you have any weepers or cuts, utilise the alum block and/or styptic pencil; use the alum for weepers and styptic pencil for cuts. Leave to dry for a couple of minutes or so and reapply if necessary.**
11	**Splash cold running water over your face and neck.**
12	**Dab, don't wipe, your face dry on a clean towel.**
13	**Splash aftershave on all the shaved areas. This might sting!**
14	**Apply shaving balm to your face to keep it hydrated.**

Artisan Products

Artisan Products

There is a growing number of artisans creating wonderful products for traditional wet shavers. Now that you are firmly wedged down the Rabbit Hole, you'll probably want to add artisan products to your collection. Below and on the next page are some examples of brushes made by Graeme Fraser, who owns and runs ShedEleven in Scotland, UK. Graeme gave me invaluable advice when I was writing this book.

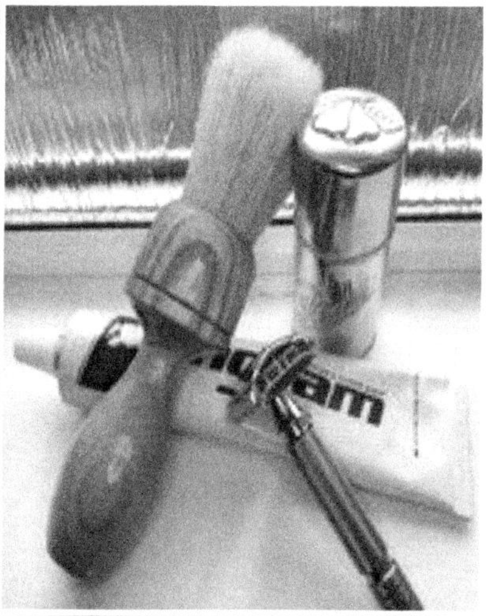

11
ShedEleven
Hand Carved Shaving Brushes

Printed in Great Britain
by Amazon

75704865R00054